NO FANCY GOODS, HAND LUGGAGE ONLY

Ellen Maria McFarlane

ATHENA PRESS
LONDON

NO FANCY GOODS, HAND LUGGAGE ONLY
Copyright © Ellen Maria McFarlane 2003

All Rights Reserved

No part of this book may be reproduced in any form
by photocopying or by any electronic or mechanical means,
including information storage and retrieval systems,
without permission in writing from both the copyright
owner and the publisher of this book.

ISBN 1 84401 147 X

First Published 2003 by
ATHENA PRESS
Queen's House, 2 Holly Road
Twickenham TW1 4EG

Printed for Athena Press

NO FANCY GOODS, HAND
LUGGAGE ONLY

*My memoirs written for my Children,
Patricia, Sheila, Lesley, Stephen and Heidi,
And my Grandchildren,
Adam, Luke, Joshua, Rebecca Natalie, Ashley, Shannon And
James
With much love*

Contents

Chapter One
My Early Childhood 7

Chapter Two
Winter Sport in East Germany 29

Chapter Three
The War Years 1939–1945 38

Chapter Four
Leaving Kanth 48

Chapter Five
The Night of 13–14 February 1945 57

Chapter Six
The End of the War 73

Chapter Seven
Martha's Ordeal 84

Chapter One
My Early Childhood

When my father was a young and newly qualified lawyer, he went with his mother to the Riesengebirge (the Giant Mountain Range in East Germany). There he met my mother, who was also spending her holiday there with her mother. They came from Dresden, where my mother was a Grammar School teacher.

My father fell in love with this pretty young lady, and all through their holiday my grandmother was the chaperone. I do not know details of their courtship, but two years later they got married. For their honeymoon they went back to the Riesengebirge, where they had met. They stayed in the same hotel, which was strangely called Die Brot Bude (The Bread Inn). My parents renamed it Die Braut Bude (The Bride Inn.)

Two years later I was born. My father really wanted a son, so, when two years later my sister Ingrid was born, he didn't seem too excited. When one of my father's friends asked him, 'What is it this time?' he scowled, 'Oh, just the usual' – just another girl.

My father was tall, dark and handsome with blue eyes and an air of authority about him, which made us not only respect him, but also very afraid of him, afraid of crossing him. Not that he would hit us, that wasn't necessary, we didn't dare be naughty. He only had to look at us. His word was law at home, as it was in his office and in court.

We lived in Kanth, a town about twenty kilometres from Breslau, the Capital of Schlesien (Selicia). We lived in a large villa, my parents, Ingrid and I, and Martha, our housekeeper and another maid. In the front of the villa was a garden with flowers and a low wall and some shrubs, but the back garden was enormous. In the middle was a lawn with an apple tree. I shall always remember us being afraid to touch the apples on that tree. There were pathways around it and flowerbeds. Further back

Chapter One
My Early Childhood

were lots of fruit trees and a large play area with a swing and a seesaw. In the hut the garden furniture was kept. All around the garden were lots of lilac trees. Surrounding everything was a low brick wall with a wrought iron fence built into the bricks, and a high wrought iron gate.

Behind our garden were some fields and houses with lots more lilac trees. Kanth was called 'The Lilac Town'. In people's gardens and along the roads and avenues lilac trees were growing and made a wonderful sight when in full bloom.

Ingrid and I used to love playing at the back of the garden, in the play area. Sometimes we hid under the fruit trees and gorged ourselves on the fruit, we liked the plums especially. But did we suffer afterwards!

Blood Sunday 1933

It was a warm and sunny Sunday afternoon. We were all in the back garden. Ingrid and I were splashing about in a zinc bathtub. My parents and Martha's sister Ida were with us, sitting in deckchairs. Martha had the day off, so, usually Ida took her place. Suddenly there was a loud commotion and shouting coming from the fields. We heard some shots being fired. My mother grabbed me whilst Ida got hold of Ingrid. They rushed us, dripping wet, into the house.

This episode happened just after Hitler came to power, and fighting had broken out because of it. We were too young to understand what it was all about, but thought it quite exciting, especially as we were put into our parents' bedroom instead of the nursery.

A wounded man tried to climb over the fence to get away from the fighting. My father quickly went back down to the back of the garden and unlocked the gate. He helped the man into the house and gave him first aid. Martha arrived home soon after and told my parents all about it. She had also been caught up in the fighting.

We always called our mother '*Mutti*' and our father '*Vati*'. Our grandmother we called '*Oma*'. Vati was very strict, but also very kind and good-natured. Yet he had some strange ideas about raising children. A strict disciplinarian, he used to admonish us.

Mutti aged about 18 months

Mutti aged 8

My Grandfather Opa Nixdorf and Mutti aged about 10

Mutti

Vati

Our Church in Kanth

Chapter One
My Early Childhood

'We Hennigs do not show our emotions on our faces.' He would correct us if we laughed too much, giggled or cried. Smiling was fine, and a thoughtful expression, but nothing 'excessive'.

Growing Up

We were never allowed to play out, that would have been unheard of. Whatever friends we made at school were thoroughly scrutinized. We only really had friends, who were the children of our parents' friends. Ingrid and I got on well together, though occasionally we squabbled, but as soon as a 'grown-up' saw us 'fighting', we pretended that nothing was wrong and quickly cuddled.

Every Sunday morning we had to go to church. Our parents went to High Mass, while Ingrid and I had to go to the Children's Mass at 11 o'clock. On Sundays we were also allowed to have dinner with our parents in the dining room, while during the week we had our meals in the nursery.

The dining room was beautiful, a large mahogany table stood in the centre of the room, surrounded by eight high-backed chairs with ornamental carvings. Along the walls were a mahogany sideboard and two glass cabinets with beautiful crystal glasses and ornaments, elaborate vases and Dresden and Meissen china. On the walls were valuable oil paintings. There was also a beautiful painting of my mother, which had been commissioned when she was about twenty-two. We loved that room, and felt very important to be dining with our parents. We were, of course, on our best behaviour, with perfect table manners. We were only permitted to speak when we were spoken to. Most Sunday afternoons our parents took us for long walks along the river Weisstritz in our 'Sunday best'.

I remember my first day at school. I don't know why Mutti didn't take me herself, but Martha took me to school. When teacher had shown all the children to their seats, the mothers (and Martha) stood by the walls around the classroom. After the names were read out, all the grown-ups went home.

When the first day at school finished and it was at last time to go home, we quietly walked to the gate, where all the parents were waiting. Mutti and Martha were there with a big colourful

Chapter One
My Early Childhood

cone-shaped thick paper bag with a frill round the top. Inside were sweets and chocolate. It was a German custom, on the first day of school, for every child to receive one of those cones. School hours were from 8 'till 12 noon, and later from 7 'till 1 p.m.

One day our teacher asked the children what their fathers did (meaning what profession our fathers had.). The children gave their various answers to the best of their knowledge. When it was my turn, teacher said, 'Ellmi, what does your father do?' Well, she knew my family, and that my father was Dr jur. Wolfgang Hennig, a well-known lawyer. I was somewhat perplexed. What does my father do? 'He rides a motorbike,' I said proudly. I should have said, 'He is *Rechtsanwalt und Notar*.'

Although we had Martha, our housekeeper, another maid and also a daily cleaner, Ingrid and I had to do our certain jobs. We always had to keep our nursery tidy, make our own beds, and every day after dinner we had to do the drying-up. That's when we developed 'trouble' with our bladders. We made a beeline to the loo, hoping that the drying-up would be done in the meantime.

Vati didn't show us much affection, but I always felt that Ingrid was his favourite. She used to climb on his lap, while I quietly waited, hoping he would want me on his lap, too. He adored my mother. She was the most important person in his life, while we came way back in second place.

Vati had one of the first cars in Kanth, an open top Opel (Vauxhall). Though we had a chauffeur, Vati and Mutti would sometimes take us out in the car. Ingrid and I would sit in the back. We were real show-offs, hoping to be seen. But Vati's main interest was his motorbike. Sometimes, when he had to go to near-by villages, he used to take Ingrid on the pillion.

One day Vati came into the playroom and said to me, 'She doesn't sit still. Let's see if you can sit still.'

I climbed onto the back of the motorbike. I was so nervous. I hardly dared to breathe. I wanted so much to please him and *sit still*. Was I relieved, when, after our return, he just said, 'Well done.' I had passed the test!

One Sunday, after lunch, Vati asked us what the priest had

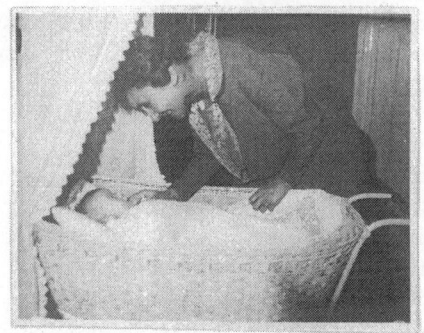

Mutti with me aged 9 weeks

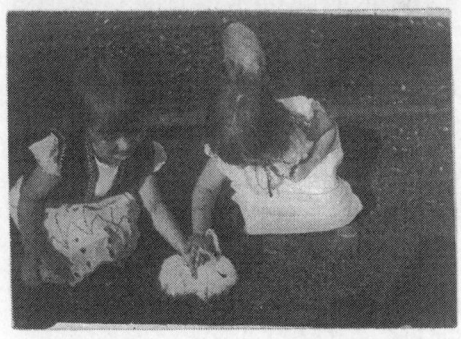

Me (on left) with Ingrid

Chapter One
My Early Childhood

talked about in his sermon. We had no idea. We hadn't really taken much notice. Vati got quite angry at our silence. 'Well? Answer me. What have you learned?'

Eventually I thought of a suitable answer and said, quite confidently, 'He talked about the sin.'

Vati was not so easily satisfied.

'What did he say about the sin?' he wanted to know.

We were in utter despair for a suitable reply until (please remember that my father was a lawyer and we had picked up some of the terminology) Ingrid burst out, 'He argued the case against it.'

Vati threw his serviette onto the tablecloth and left the room. We were quite worried, but relieved, when he came back a short while later. He didn't say any more. I think he left the room, because he didn't want us to see him laughing. From then on, we had to give a weekly account of what the priest had preached on Sunday.

Festive Seasons in Germany

Easter is no doubt celebrated the same as anywhere else. When the weather was warm enough the eggs were hidden in the garden. It took us some time to find them, as it was a big garden, but it was always very exciting.

Even more special was Christmas. We eagerly looked forward to Christmas Eve. In the morning we helped Martha decorate the tree with wax candles and lots of colourful decorations. Later we were allowed to help Vati make the 'Punch'. Christmas and New Year were the only times Vati spent in the kitchen, to make the 'Punch'.

We rubbed lots of sugar cubes on the washed skins of oranges 'till they turned a lovely orange colour. These sugar cubes were put into a crystal punch bowl. Cinnamon and some other spices were added. Then Vati poured brandy and some white wine into the bowl, and lastly some bottled strawberries. It looked and smelled so delicious, but we weren't allowed even a tiny taste. We were given the juice of the fruit instead.

At about 6 o'clock in the evening a little bell rang. That was the signal to go to the dining room. The door was open, but we

Chapter One
My Early Childhood

weren't allowed to enter. First we had to sing a Christmas carol with Martha's help, while Mutti played the Carol on the piano. Then we entered.

The table was laid with a white damask tablecloth, silver cutlery, linen serviettes and lovely Christmas decorations and two silver candelabra. The wax candles were lit and also the ones on the tree.

While we took our places, Ingrid and I nudged each other. We could see through the open sliding doors to the lounge, several armchairs covered with white sheets. We knew our presents were hidden under those sheets. But first we had to have our meal.

Every year the traditional supper for Christmas and New Year's Eve was the same: *Weisswuerstchen* (very tasty sausages, which the butchers in East Germany specially prepared for this time of year only.) With that we had potatoes, Sauerkraut and a delicious Polish gravy, a special Polish recipe.

After the meal we all went into the lounge and opened our presents, including Martha. We always had lovely presents. One, which I remember always, was the enormous doll's house with several rooms – hallway, staircase, bathroom and bedrooms – all lit up with little lights and table lamps. In the kitchen were a cooker, sink, table and chairs. There were lots of dishes with tiny food items, all made out of marzipan, like fruit, eggs, bread and potatoes.

It was that Christmas that we lost our budgie, Hansel. We meant well and spoilt him with some of the goodies, but the next morning he was dead. We were terribly upset – he had been so tame. He was always flying about in the nursery, often sitting on our fingers or our head.

Another Christmas I was given a zither. I always loved music. I was very excited and practiced hard. We often enjoyed musical evenings, Mutti played the piano, I played the zither and Ingrid the flute. Sometimes Ingrid and I would sing duets, accompanied by Mutti on the piano.

The four Sundays before Christmas were also important. A small wreath made from fir tree branches was suspended from the ceiling, and decorated with small baubles, red bows and tinsel, and four wax candles. On the fourth Sunday before Christmas

Chapter One
My Early Childhood

one of the candles was lit, for a while. On the third Sunday before Christmas two candles were lit, on the second Sunday three candles were lit and on the last Sunday before Christmas all four candles were lit, the first ones having been replaced.

The 6th of December, St Nicolas Day, is a special day for young children. A male relative or friend dresses up as Father Christmas and goes to the family, carrying a sack over his shoulder and a besom, (a broom, made by tying a bundle of twigs together). He would then ask the parents, if the child in question had been good all year. If not, he would threaten the child with the besom, or even slightly smack a boy with it. But he always gave the children some little present out of the sack – sweets, chocolate and nuts, maybe even a small toy.

I was always called 'Ellmi' (that is putting both my Christian names together: 'Ell' from Ellen and 'mi' from Maria. This was my father's wish, because my mother's name was Ellen, and I was not to be called the same name. He adored my mother, but Ingrid and I were not very important.

I remember the one and only time Vati hit me. Ingrid had scribbled my name on the side of the kitchen table, where we sometimes had our breakfast. When Vati found out, he assumed that I had done it, because Ingrid had just started school. I denied doing it. Vati accused me of lying and smacked me. I fell off the little chair I was sitting on. Ingrid was very upset and told Vati that she had done the writing. Vati told Ingrid not to do it again, and to me he said, 'A smack for nothing won't do you any harm.'

For our birthdays we were always asked by Martha what we would like to have for dinner. We could choose our favourite meal. Ingrid chose Knackwurst (a very tasty sausage similar to a Frankfurter, only bigger) with potatoes and a mustard gravy. I chose macaroni with ham and grated cheese on top.

Although I was older than my sister, she was taller than me (she still is). I was a poor eater, while Ingrid had a good appetite. We always had to eat everything that was put in front of us. Ingrid had no problems, but for me mealtimes were always a dreaded task. I was not allowed to leave the table until my plate was empty. Sometimes it took hours (this is not exaggerated), especially when we had spinach, to which Martha added '*grieven*'. She fried small

Chapter One
My Early Childhood

cut up cubes of pork fat in a frying pan until all the fat was separated and small lumps of brown and crispy bits remained. Those bits (*grieven*) she mixed into the spinach. Already, when I smelled the *grieven* frying, my stomach would turn over – the smell alone made me feel sick.

It was the same with custard or thick soup, which had lumps in. We weren't allowed to push the lumps or *grieven* to the side of the plate. Ingrid was much braver than I. She felt sorry for me when Mutti held my nose shut and I had to open my mouth to breathe. Mutti shovelled the food in my mouth, again and again, at the same time trying to make me swallow it, until I was actually sick. There was nothing worse than having to eat that stuff.

Once, when no one was looking, I put my whole mouthful of spinach into my hankie. We always wore pinafores with pockets, and I was able to dispose of the pinafore in the wash basket. When Martha found the disgusting green hankie in the wash the next day, she didn't tell my mother. But when she found little earthworms and ladybirds wriggling in my pockets one day, which I had lovingly collected, she had enough. I was not only told off, but I had to empty my pockets in the garden and wash the pinafore myself.

My grandmother, Oma Nixdorf

We called my grandmother 'Oma'. She was a very active and energetic lady, very fond of all kinds of sport. We adored her. She taught us to swim, ride a bike, table tennis, skiing and even ice-skating. She was tall and slim, and, although very athletic and adventurous, she was always very elegant.

We loved going to Oma's house in Dresden-Neustadt. Her father, our Grandfather Winkler, had been a Master builder and Architect. He had erected many beautiful buildings in Dresden, with sculptures and ornaments, for which Dresden was famous. Most of the properties and his fortune were lost in the inflation of the 1920s. Only the building in Glacis-Strasse (Oma's house) withstood the financial crash of 1929.

It was a huge corner building with ten big shop windows. There was a baker and a hair salon. I cannot remember the other shops. The building was five storeys high. The entrance was on

My Grandmother Oma Nixdorf

Oma's House in Dresden

Rewahl on the East Sea, 1935

Chapter One
My Early Childhood

the corner. A large hallway and wide staircase led up to the apartments on either side. Oma's apartment was on the second floor, large rooms with Persian carpets and antique furniture. We were always happy staying with Oma. Not only because she spoilt us, but also she was our idol, we adored her.

Dresden was a most beautiful and exciting town. At night we used to lay awake in bed, just listening to the traffic, the sound of trams going past, and watching the tram-lights reflecting along the ceiling.

Oma used to take us on lovely holidays. I shall always remember the holiday to a village in the Sudetenland. I have forgotten the name. We stayed on a farm. The owners were friends of Oma's. Moving about in the stables, touching the horses, pigs and cows was a new and very exciting experience for us, especially as we were allowed to help (or rather try) to milk the cows.

After that we were shown how to make the butter. The milk was poured into a wooden churn, which was then firmly shut and placed on a stand. Standing on either side, we got hold of a handle each, and then we shook the churn to-and-fro until the butter was separated from the liquid. This liquid, the *Molken*, was at the bottom of the churn. The home baked bread and fresh butter was delicious. One thing though, I was made to drink some of the *Molken* and buttermilk and goat's milk. Yuck. But it was not as bad as spinach and lumpy soup.

While there, we also went to a Lido. Ingrid, as usual, was swimming like a fish. I didn't like going into the deep end. I used to get terribly out of breath. I preferred being near the bars on the side of the pool.

Ingrid kept calling me to join her; she was in the middle of the pool holding on to a big log. I didn't want to look like a coward in front of the other children in the water, so I let go of the bar and swam to Ingrid. Just then the log kept rolling and I couldn't get a grip. I panicked and quickly turned around to swim back. I was so exhausted and out of breath that I went under. A young man jumped in and helped me out. I was terribly embarrassed. After that incident I wouldn't go back to the Lido in case someone recognized me.

Chapter One
My Early Childhood

Pommern 1935

Mutti, Oma and some friends of Oma's came with us on a holiday to the Ostsee (East Sea). We went to Rewahl in Pommern and stayed in the Hotel Duenenhof from the 3rd to the 29th of July 1935. The Duenenhof was a big hotel right by the sea. We had a lovely view from our windows overlooking the ocean. Ingrid and I couldn't wait to run down the wide terrace steps to the beach every morning.

One day, Oma was sitting in the deckchair, Ingrid was already in the water, while I was just playing in the sand and letting the water run over my feet. Suddenly a huge wave grabbed me and I disappeared under the water. I remember so clearly crawling out on all fours, almost in tears. My face must have been a picture, and soon we had a laugh about it. After that incident I was even more wary of wide areas of water.

When Oma came to visit us in Kanth, she came most times on her motorbike, instead of the train. She said it was much quicker and nicer. Once she had an accident and broke her arm. That didn't stop her getting back on her motorbike a few weeks later.

On one of her visits we were all getting ready to go out. The saying is that women take longer to get ready. Well, Vati wasn't ready, so Oma went to his room, knocked on the door and called out, 'Wolfgang, have you shaved yet?'

My father's prompt reply was, 'No, have you?'

Oma was quite indignant about his response, but Vati was always a bit of a tease and a joker.

Oma must have been well into her sixties, when she went for her first flight. She hired a small two-seater plane, a Junkers J1 Commercial Biplane. She had arranged to fly from Dresden to Breslau via Kanth. She was going to fly over the area we lived. We knew the exact time and waited on the flat part of our roof, which had a balustrade around it for safety. When we saw the plane we waved like mad with our white towels. We saw two people in the plane.

When the daughter of one of Oma's friends got married, we were asked to be 'flower girls'. We didn't like the idea very much, as we didn't know the people and thought we were a bit too old to be 'flower girls'. Special dresses were made for us, and a visit to the

Dresden, The Zwinger (Wallpavillion)

Chapter One
My Early Childhood

hairdresser transformed our hair. My long plaits were changed into long curly tresses, while Ingrid's short hair was curled on top. In one hand we carried a basket of flower petals, while with the other hand we threw them along the aisle in front of the young couple.

The next day, as a special treat, Oma and Ur-Oma Winkler (our Great Grandmother) took us to see our first opera: *Haensel und Gretel* and *Die Puppenfee* (The Doll's Fairy) by Engelbert Humperding (the composer, not the singer!).

Ur-Oma Winkler was a wonderful old lady, and, although well into her eighties, she was still very active. She enjoyed going out. Again, dressed in our finery, we all set off to the Dresden Opera House.

The approach to the opera house was already very impressive. Ladies in beautiful evening dresses, accompanied by their fine gentlemen, arrived in cars or horse drawn carriages. High above the main entrance was a colossal bronze sculpture, depicting Ariadne and Dionysus in a carriage drawn by two panthers. Ariadne, according to Greek Mythology, was the daughter of Minos, King of Crete, and Pasiphae. Ariadne fell in love with Theseus, who had gone to Crete to kill the Minotaur. But sadly there was no romance. After Theseus killed the Minotaur, he left Crete. Ariadne eventually married Dionysus, the son of Zeus.

On either side of the tower-like structure of the main building were the carved images of Goethe and Schiller (the German poets). There were many more statues and carvings to be seen.

As we entered the foyer, the splendour and atmosphere were breathtaking. Huge chandeliers were suspended from the ceiling. On the walls were large paintings in ornamental frames, and mirrors surrounded by draped velvet curtains. The crystal wall-lights were lit and cast a romantic hue over the paintings. We were filled with awe, while mingling with all these elegant people.

I loved hearing the sound of the instruments being tuned. In the intermission between the two operas, we strolled in the foyer and sat in the plush armchairs. As we walked back to our seats, listening to the tuning of the instruments, we felt quite grown-up. It was an unforgettable experience, and it was the music that made me decide that I wanted to be an opera singer when I grew up.

A view of Dresden.

Chapter One
My Early Childhood

Back at Oma's flat I played the melodies on the piano with my right hand, making up the accompaniment with my left. Ingrid and I would sing some of the tunes from the opera.

Auntie Erna (my other Godmother) was a dear friend of Mutti's. She lived in Dresden-Radebeul. When we went to see her, she had just had a fall and broken her leg. I was quite pleased to be able to help and water her garden.

Dresden, the capital city of Saxony, was no doubt the most beautiful city in Germany. For many centuries, the Saxon princes had shaped a city centre by extending the activities of their palaces and building a realm of galleries, gardens and museums, as well as theatres and beautiful churches. Several bridges over the river Elbe connected the Neustadt to the Altstadt. Exquisite Baroque palaces were built in Dresden-Altstadt. Near the opera house in Dresden-Neustadt was the *Zwinger* (Wall Pavilion), a most elaborate combination of buildings, sculptures and fountains. The gardens were a mass of blooms.

Dresden was a vision!

There was also a resident circus in Dresden, a large permanent building in the shape of a huge tent. I loved going to the circus. The animals, the clowns and the music all fascinated me. I admired the beautifully clad artists on the trapeze and on horseback. It was then that I decided I was not going to be an opera singer, but a circus performer instead, an acrobatic horse rider. What dreams I had!

I did have great imagination and, after seeing my first silent film in Kanth, I was determined to become a scriptwriter. I made up lovely stories. One was about a Hungarian prince, who fell in love with a circus performer, a high-flying trapeze artist.

Poetry was definitely my favourite subject. I enjoyed writing limericks. It was one of my poems, which got me into serious trouble in school, because I had made fun of one of our teachers. But I thought it harmless fun. All my classmates read it and enjoyed it. Although the poem was in German, I'll try and make it up in English. It was something like this:

Chapter One
My Early Childhood

> Of all the teachers in our town,
> Our teacher is just like a clown.
> His hair is thick
> His nose too big
> And his mouth a permanent frown.
>
> God help you, if you make him cross,
> You'll soon find out, who is the boss.
> He'll want to shout,
> But nought comes out,
> For words he's at a loss.
>
> Our teacher's name is Dr May,
> He's short and stocky, I must say.
> He carries his belly
> Like a wobbly jelly.
> Don't tell him, I said so, I pray.

I don't think the German version was quite as strongly worded, it was just meant to be funny. Anyway, when I got found out I was in serious trouble. I got severely reprimanded by our headmaster and had to apologise to the teacher in front of the whole school. Dr May was not a very popular teacher, and everything I wrote was true, but I know I shouldn't have done it. When he got annoyed with anyone, he really wanted to shout, but couldn't get the words out. Then he almost used to foam at the mouth.

The slightest thing made him angry. Once, when the girl I shared the bench with sat a little too far over my side, he grabbed her by the arm and pulled her over so hard, that she fell on the floor. A few weeks later, Dr May left our school.

Our First Holy Communion

As we were Roman Catholics, we went to our first Holy Communion at an early age. Every Saturday afternoon we had to go to our lessons, until the big day arrived. Dressed in our specially made white dresses, wearing a Crucifix on a gold chain and a garland of daisies in our hair, we felt very important. In one

On our first Holy Communion

In Dresden ready to go to the Opera

Our first holy Communion

Chapter One
My Early Childhood

hand we held the Holy Bible and in the other a large candle. My Godmothers were Auntie Charlotte from Dresden-Altstadt and Auntie Erna from Dresden-Radebeul. It is important that I am telling you about my two Godmothers, because I have to tell you about their fate in a later chapter.

After the church service we had a party at home, and lots of presents from relatives, and especially from our Godmothers. These presents were mainly solid silver cutlery for our 'Bottom-drawer'. Every following year for birthdays and Christmas we received more silver cutlery, always the same engraved design and our initials, to add to our collection for the 'Bottom-drawer'. That, I think, was the custom in Germany.

From then on, Ingrid and I had to go to confession every month. What a problem that sometimes was, trying to think what sins we had committed. We racked our brains. We had to come up with something by next Saturday.

We decided to arrange some mischief. We made a nuisance phone call to the chemist and ordered a couple of items, some tablets and cream (under a false name). When we asked the chemist if he could also send some 'pickled cellar-steps', we burst out laughing and put the phone down quickly. What idiots we were, but at least we had another sin to add to the' occasional squabble.

Mutti belonged to a Ladies Club. Meetings were usually held in one of the lady's houses. When it was Mutti's turn for the meeting to be held in our house, Ingrid and I were always very pleased. It meant we could stay up a little longer and join the grown-ups for coffee and cake for a while, though Ingrid and I did not get the 'real' coffee. We were always given *Ersatz Kaffee*. The ladies took turns to read from a book aloud, while some of the others did needlework or knitting, while listening. Every week the ladies continued reading the next chapter of their book, wherever the meeting was held.

A view of the River Weintritz near Kanth.

Chapter Two
Winter Sport in East Germany

Winter in East Germany meant lots of snow, several months of snow. The weather was cold and crisp, yet between 12 noon and 2 in the afternoon the sun made the air quite mild, but not warm enough to melt the snow. We loved building snowmen and having snowball fights.

When we were younger, Martha used to take us shopping on a sledge, all wrapped up warm. Although it was already dark, the snow made it look quite bright. It was very exciting, especially when she took us Christmas shopping and to see all the lights and Christmas decorations.

One year one of my Christmas presents was a violin. It's difficult to describe my excitement. I had hoped for one for a long time, being an ardent admirer of Yehudi Menuin. Now my dream had come true, I owned a violin! I soon had lessons with a well-known lady teacher. I really practiced hard and enjoyed it. I don't know about my parents, Ingrid or Martha or anyone else in our household, they must have suffered earache at times!

One of our favourite winter sports was ice-skating on our frozen lake. This lake in our local park was always tested first, before any children were allowed onto it. Ingrid and I set off, dressed up warm and our skates hanging over our shoulders. At the lake we met lots of our school friends. We had a great time, racing each other, doing jumps and spins, skating backwards, and pretending to be like Sonja Henjee. Well nothing like her, but we enjoyed ourselves.

Many years later, when I took one of my children ice-skating, I had a go myself and could hardly skate in a straight line. It's strange, how you lose your confidence.

Skiing was not only another winter sport, but very useful to get around in thick snow. From the age of ten, all children had to

Chapter Two
Winter Sport in East Germany

join the *Hitler Jugend* (Hitler Youth). For the boys it was called '*Jungvolk*' and for the girls '*Jungmaedchen*'. When, after some time, I was made a leader of a '*Schaft*', a small group of girls in a nearby village, the skis came in very handy in winter. Once a week in the afternoon I put on my skis and crossed the fields to the village. There was an old gallows by the roadside, or more or less the remains of an old gallows. It may not have been used for a hundred years or more, but I always had an eerie feeling passing it. That's why I went over the fields instead.

Every meeting started with a short prayer. Then the latest news items were discussed briefly. We sang patriotic songs and folksongs. Knitting scarves and blankets for the soldiers was also on the agenda, and making toys for poor children. We used fretsaws to cut patterns out of three-ply wood and made some lovely little toys, which we painted and glued and screwed together, like puppets on a string and mobiles, doll's cradles and many more. I remember especially the little rocking horse I made. All these toys went to the local orphanage.

We also did marching and a lot of sport in summer, collecting and destroying may beetles and potato bugs. Helping the farmers in the fields were also very important activities.

Once a year was a big sports meeting of all the Hitler Youth of Kanth and surrounding villages, on the sports field in Kanth. It was usually a hot day, and standing to attention for any length of time was quite exhausting. The children looked very smart in their black skirts and white blouses, and black scarves with brown leather toggles. The leaders had pleated leather straps hanging from the toggle to the shoulder buttons, the colour being dependent on the rank of the person. Mine was green.

The events included long distance races around the sports field, relay races and long and high jumps. Throwing balls or javelins was not my best point, my arm felt as if it was dislocated. I preferred long jumps and high jumps. My favourite activity was gymnastics.

Moving House

When Mutti decided to move from our lovely home to another villa, we were very disappointed. We loved our home. We didn't

At our new house looking out from the veranda

With our Great Grandmother Ur-Oma Winkler

Me with Oma

Chapter Two
Winter Sport in East Germany

want to move, but in the end we did our best to help. Our new home in Bahnhof Strasse (Station Road) was nice, but the garden was not as big. There were fruit trees, bushes and vegetable patches, but no proper play area. Around the house were flowerbeds and shrubs. In the front was a lawn, surrounded by pathways, flowers and trees. There was a glass veranda on the front of the house with steps leading up to it.

During the first night in our new home, when everybody was asleep, there was suddenly a terrific crash. It sounded like some burglar had climbed in and fallen over the glass cabinet. My parents, Martha and Ingrid, armed with torch, hammer and broom, crept gingerly from room to room, to investigate. Then they saw what had happened: the chandelier in Vati's private lounge (we called it the 'smokers' room') had crashed down onto the round brass table with a large glass ashtray. The table had fallen over, and glass from the chandeliers and ashtray was everywhere.

I slept through all the noise and commotion, but, when everybody was sitting in the lounge next to my bedroom, I woke up from the whispering. They were amazed that I hadn't heard all the noise, but had heard their whispers. Martha explained what had happened. The chandelier was too heavy for the hooks on the ceiling. The electrician's apprentice had used the wrong hooks.

Sometimes my friend Ursula was allowed to come and play with us. We dressed up as Cowboys and Indians. Old pyjamas were made into 'authentic' Indian costumes by stitching fringes onto the outer legs and sleeves. The hair from some old dolls we used as scalps around our waist like trophies of the Indian chiefs. We tied a ribbon round our foreheads and stuck some duck feathers into the back of the ribbon. One of Vati's old pipes was our 'peace pipe'.

We made a hole in the ground and lit a fire in it with paper and small twigs, over which we placed a metal grid. The baked potatoes we cooked in the fire weren't very nice, they tasted sooty and burnt, and the semolina, which we cooked on top of the grid, had lumps in it. That was the last time we cooked semolina – it was noodles instead, with cheese on top.

With crossed legs we sat round the fire and pretended to

Chapter Two
Winter Sport in East Germany

smoke the peace pipe. Ingrid was usually the Indian chief 'Winnetou', Ursula was 'Running Bear', while I was Winnetou's friend, the cowboy 'Old Shatterhand'.

'There is a white squaw carrying a basket,' said Running Bear, pointing at Martha when she came into the garden to hang out the washing.

All these names and ideas we got from the books we used to read, which were at the time every child's craze, written by the author Karl May (no relation to my teacher). He wrote over sixty volumes, mostly about the Indians, their struggles against the white settlers and their fights with other tribes. Those were most gripping tales of heroism and adventures. Yet Karl May had never been to any of the places he so vividly described. He was quite old, when, for the first time, he sat foot in America, Canada and Egypt, where he collected all the memorabilia, which are exhibited in the Karl May Museum in Dresden-Radebeul.

He spent his last years in the 'Villa Shatterhand' – named after the hero of his stories about the Red Indians. Winnetou was the Apache Chief and definitely every child's favourite Indian. The cowboy, Old Shatterhand, was his faithful friend.

We enjoyed reconstructing the adventures written in his books. Sometimes one of us was tied to the 'stake'. For that we used the wooden post, part of the framework in our back garden, used for beating carpets. There were no vacuum cleaners in those days, only carpet sweepers.

Martha Meets Richard

Whenever some painting and decorating needed to be done, Mutti employed a young man by the name of Richard Fleischer. He was a very nice man. Ingrid and I were very fond of him. Martha and Richard soon became a couple. At weekends they often took Ingrid and me out with them in the afternoon, to the park or to the pictures.

Martha and Richard got married in 1939, just before he was called up and joined the infantry. When Martha was expecting their first baby, she left our household and a girl called Frieda took her place. She joined Hanna, our daily help. Martha got a nice flat in a large block of flats near the station, but she came to

Chapter Two
Winter Sport in East Germany

see us often, or we spent some time in her flat. Looking out from her kitchen window, we could overlook our road, the Bahnhof Strasse.

Nine months after their wedding, at which we were bridesmaids, (not flower girls), Martha gave birth to a little girl. She named her Ingrid. I wanted to be Godmother, but unfortunately I was too young. Ingrid was a lovely little baby with blond hair and blue eyes. My sister Ingrid and I often took her out in the pram for walks.

My violin lessons went so well, that I was soon sent to Breslau to a very well known violinist for lessons. He told Mutti that, if I continued to make such good progress, I would one day become a great violinist. This was not to be, as I will explain later.

I was always very fond of anything to do with art, whether it was music, drawing or handicrafts, I was, naturally, not particularly interested in my other lessons in school. I was good at math, not bad in French and Latin, but some lessons like Science, Religious Education and 'English' I could have done without. Our English teacher was a typical old spinster and her lessons were very boring.

Quite often she came to our house to see my parents, to have a good moan about me not being a star pupil, or telling them something I was supposed to have done wrong. No doubt she just liked coming to our house. Ingrid and I didn't like her very much, and we tried to avoid her, when we knew she was coming. She usually stayed for coffee and cake, and we were then expected to join the grown-ups, much to our dismay.

We went to the local private Pedagogue, a boy's Grammar school in Kanth, as there was no girl's Grammar school in our town. The nearest one was in Breslau. My class in Kanth consisted of four girls and twelve boys. All my classmates were great. We were a good team. Whenever one of us did something wrong, and the class was asked who did the certain misdeed, the whole class would stand up. Usually it was nothing serious and the whole matter was overlooked, or the whole class was punished. Then we all had to write pages and pages of certain works by Schiller or Goethe.

Chapter Two
Winter Sport in East Germany

The Flood

One year we had an enormous amount of snowfall. When the weather got milder the snow melted and the water came in torrents down from the mountains in the Riesengebirge. Our local river, the Weisstritz, overflowed and Kanth was completely under water.

Ingrid was the first one to look out of the window in the morning, and called me to look at the river outside our house. The street, our garden, everything was under water. We couldn't go to school, which I found very exciting, but Ingrid was disappointed. She loved school.

Our cellar was knee deep under water, the coal was floating about, our bikes and skies were standing in water. Luckily the water hadn't quite reached the shelves with all the preserves and other food items, but everything else on the floor, like sacks of potatoes and bundles of firewood, were completely spoiled.

We lived slightly higher up, but the poor people, who lived nearer to the river, must have had a much worse time. Some people were getting about in canoes, while others waded through the water. Martha put on her wellies and went shopping. When she came back, her feet were soaked. The water was higher than her wellies. Slowly, over the next few days, the water subsided and after the clean up and drying out, everything went back to normal.

Once a year the carnival came to Kanth. That was always very exciting. On the *Schuetzen Wiese*, the open grassland near the river, dozens of stalls and many carousels were erected. There was always a lot of activity when we met our school friends there. The rifle range was one of my favourites. By nine o'clock at night we had to be home.

One evening, Hans, who was a year older than me and in a class above mine at school, joined me at the rifle range. He was quite a good shot and although I beat him, I think he let me win. He walked me home, as he had to get to the station. By my front gate, he kissed me. I was quite embarrassed and quickly disappeared indoors. I must have been very silly, but after that (my first kiss) I tried to avoid bumping into him again. As he came to school by train, he had to pass my house to get to the

Hans and Auntie Erna's House.

Chapter Two
Winter Sport in East Germany

station. I couldn't avoid letting him walk me home sometimes. Hans was a very nice boy. He was also in the Hitler Youth. I think it was compulsory for all children to belong to the Hitler Youth. One day he gave me a photo. I wonder now, what happened to him since the war?

Chapter Three
The War Years 1939–1945

Ur-Oma Winkler died at the age of eighty-nine in 1938. Until three days before her death she was fit and well. She had just finished knitting scarves for Ingrid and me. We treasured those scarves for many years.

My father had been a young officer in the Luftwaffe in the First World War. He was still in the reserves and every second year he had to go on manoeuvres for short periods. The last time was in 1938. Now, in early August 1939, he was called up again, out of turn. This time it was not for manoeuvres, this time it meant war.

We were all very upset, especially Mutti. Mr Fleischer and our chauffeur, who also doubled as our gardener, were called up at the same time. Vati was very concerned about the political situation and warned us to be careful. Little did Ingrid and I understand why, or what was happening. Why was Vati worried and why did we have to be careful?

Public places like the Town Hall, schools and shops had to display pictures of 'the Fuehrer'. At the time we didn't understand why Vati was so against the Nazi Regime. He did not display a picture of Hitler in his office. He advised us never to make any political comments to anyone. But, after all, Hitler gave employment to the people. He built the Autobahn, and many more structures.

Hitler's promise was, 'No one shall go hungry, no one shall be cold.' People believed him. Until we realized that the Jews were being persecuted, and some of Vati's friends were Jews, we did not understand Vati's attitude. Everybody had to prove to be a pure Aryan descendant, and that none of our ancestors had Jewish blood in them.

While Mutti got very busy tracing our family history, we

Chapter Three
The War Years 1939–1945

thought it rather exciting to find out more about our ancestors. Mutti continued her search until the evidence dried up in 1702. There were many interesting people as our forefathers – doctors, landowners, lawyers, a postmaster general, architect, a Prussian general and many more. I have still got the *Stammbaum* (Family Tree) somewhere in my papers.

We knew that the Jews had to wear the Star of David. Later they disappeared. We had no idea why or where to. When, many years later, I heard about the atrocities that had been committed, I could not believe it. I could not comprehend that such terrible things had happened. The ordinary German people didn't know of the existence of those dreadful places, like Belsen and Auschwitz.

When we were young we always had to curtsey when greeting grown-ups. But later we were told in school to say 'Heil Hitler' with raised right arm. We hated doing that, it felt so stupid, little girls or adults raising their right arm and saying that greeting.

As our chauffeur had also been called up, Mutti had no option but to learn to drive. Eventually she took us on short journeys. After Vati left, Mutti was very determent for Vati's practice to stay in business. She took over the office, studied law books and dismissed the clerk, who was not very competent, and employed another typist. She arranged for another, older Barrister to come at times for important court cases and for special signatures. Everything went smoothly.

One of Vati's clients, a wealthy farmer, gave Mutti a whole live pig to be slaughtered. A butcher came to the house, and in the back yard the poor pig was killed. Ingrid and I had to stay in our room, but we realized what was going on. We were absolutely horrified.

Special sausages were made, some of the meat was smoke treated, some preserved in salt, and some Martha preserved in glass jars (*Kilner* jars). These jars were slowly boiled in a large saucepan (half filled with water), up to a certain temperature and length of time. There were no refrigerators or freezers in those days.

It was time for me to go to a higher school. Mutti had put my name down at a private Grammar school in Breslau. Every day I

Chapter Three
The War Years 1939–1945

took the train to Breslau and walked the short distance from the station to my new school. It was here that I enjoyed school most of all. I made new friends, and the teachers were very nice and made lessons most interesting.

One day after school, on my way back to the station, I noticed a board in front of a building, advertising ballet lessons. That's when I could make one of my dreams come true, I thought. But Mutti would not hear of it. Ballet lessons were out of the question. No way was I having money towards that. It was not the done thing for a young lady to have anything to do with the stage. No more was said.

I saved all my pocket money up for some time and eventually I enrolled at the ballet school. It wasn't long after that my money ran out. But I did enjoy the few lessons I had, and continued to dream of becoming a ballerina one day.

One of my friends from my previous school in Kanth was Udo. His father was a gentleman farmer and owned a large estate near Kanth. Udo was an only child and his parents were good friends of my parents. Whenever we visited them, Udo always gave me a lift on his motorbike. He was a few years older than me and quite tall and handsome.

Mutti explained to me that Udo was not in good health and had had several operations. He was not supposed to ride the short distance to Kanth on the bumpy trains, thus the motorbike. Whatever the reason, I was quite pleased getting rides on the back of his bike.

I was about fourteen when Oma took Ingrid and me to Bad Salzbrunn, a famous East German Health Resort. Our hotel was in the grounds of the Spa. In the morning we mingled with the other guests in the park before going to have our first drink of the Spa Water and then going to breakfast.

For several days I had noticed a young man watching, but I didn't give it a thought. One afternoon, Ingrid had already gone swimming, while I listened to the open-air orchestra, I remembered Ingrid was waiting for me to join her. As I walked along the path through the park, I was suddenly pulled to the side into some bushes. I didn't scream; I was too busy kicking and punching this bloke. I managed to get away and ran as fast as I could and told Oma. The park was searched, but the man had disappeared. After that incident Ingrid and I always stayed together.

Often, in the afternoons Ingrid and I sat and listened to the open-air orchestra. It was absolute magic, and so was the conductor – tall, elegant and very handsome. I had quite a crush on him, until one day, from my bedroom window, I saw him walking along the path with a beautiful lady and two small children. I felt very upset; this was my first teenage crush.

Mr Fleischer came home on leave from the army. Martha and Richard were a happy and devoted couple. Nearly every day they came to see us with their little daughter Ingrid. When, nine months later, Martha gave birth to a little boy, I was old enough to be Godmother. You have to be fourteen and now I was. I was very thrilled and had visions of really spoiling my Godchild. Martha called him Michael.

Carlsruhe 1943

Because I was smaller than Ingrid, and (supposedly) quite delicate, my mother sent me to Carlsruhe, a small country town in Oberschlesien (Higher Selicia). Mutti thought the country air and wholesome country food would make me a better eater.

I stayed on a small farm there. I didn't like it. The wife, a rather robust looking woman, always wore a dark pinafore and her hair in a bun at the back of her neck. The place looked old and gloomy, the toilet was outside in the backyard. In the kitchen was a big wooden table, where we had our meals, sitting on wooden benches.

I wondered why Mutti had sent me to this place. Was I being punished? For what? If Mutti thought the country air would do me good, why here? She didn't know this place, nor the people. It had all been arranged by phone. Our chauffeur drove me there.

One evening, we were all sitting round the table for our meal, my landlady, her husband, two daughters, a farm worker and me. We had bread and butter and homemade black treacle for supper. When it was my turn to help myself to the treacle, I got the shock of my life. With my knife I spread a big black spider on to my bread. I was nearly sick. I didn't know what to do, but, being too polite to complain (I probably would have been told to remove

Reconstruction of the School play (in the back garden in Carlsruhe)

Chapter Three
The War Years 1939–1945

the spider and eat the rest.) I pretended to feel ill. I asked to leave the table and waited in the toilet outside until I was sure the table had been cleared.

I think this incident has given me a permanent phobia of spiders.

Soon after, Mutti arranged for me to move to a small boarding house in Carlsruhe. That was much better. I lived there with three other girls from my class. We shared a large room upstairs. There were two beds along the walls on either side of the room. Under the window were a table and four chairs. The wardrobe and chest of drawers were along the end of the other wall. Near the door was an old-fashioned china basin and jug on a pedestal, under which was a bucket for the used wash water. We had to fetch the water from a well outside. The toilet was also outside in the yard.

But I liked it there, the landlady was very nice and us four girls got on very well. At night, after our homework was done, we went to bed and told each other ghost stories, real creepy ones. One night I tied a piece of string to the leg of one of the chairs, then I looped it over the door handle and back to my bed. Slowly I began to pull the string. The chair moved slowly across the room. The girls disappeared under the blankets like a flash. When I put the light on and confessed, we had a good laugh.

Our landlady, Frau Haufler, always took an interest in our progress at school. She made sure we did our homework undisturbed in our room. Our meals we had downstairs with her and her ten-year-old son, Reini. Frau Haufler told us all about her older son, Waldemar, who was in the army. She spoke of him with great pride and affection. She was looking forward to him coming home on leave soon.

It was decided to stage a play for all the school, relatives and friends. I had previously written an essay about *The Flying Suitcase*, on which a young prince, Prince Fidelius, fell asleep, and in his dreams travelled to lots of exciting places in the world. My teacher liked my story and gave me the task of producing the play.

We rehearsed in our free time after school. Everybody involved enjoyed it immensely. After several weeks and with the help of some of the mothers, who made the costumes, we were

Chapter Three
The War Years 1939–1945

ready. I played the principal part, Prince Fidelius. I shall always remember the enthusiastic applause of our audience. In one scene, sitting on my suitcase, I played a tune from *The Student Prince* on my violin and Robert Schumann's *Traeumerei*, accompanied by an older pupil on the piano. When we played *Gaudeamus igitur* the older pupils all joined in, singing the words. The play was a great success and the headmaster congratulated us all on stage.

At the beginning of March 1944, Waldemar came home on leave. He was a very good-looking young man, and ever so nice. Often in the evenings we all joined him and his Mum in the lounge. He would tell us about his exciting time in the army. The time went far too quick and Waldemar had to go back to the front. He gave me two photos. On the back he wrote:

'In remembrance of many beautiful hours spent in Carlsruhe.

Yours in Friendship, Waldemar Haufler 25.3.44'

Waldemar Haufler and Reini

Waldemar 1944 and Ingrid & I at Moehne Sea.

Chapter Three
The War Years 1939–1945

January 1945 – Nearing the End of the War.

I was home from Carlsruhe. The situation on the Eastern Front looked grim. The war everywhere was going badly. Not much was broadcast on the radio. If you wanted to listen to a special radio station, which sent propaganda messages by a Lord Haw-Haw, you had to be very careful not to get found out.

Vati had, for some time, asked Mutti to go with us to Oma's house in Dresden. He was very concerned about the whole situation and worried about our safety. Breslau was being bombed by the Russians. We could hear the bombs exploding in the distance. The sounds no doubt came from the Soviet Katyusha rockets, but I'm not sure.

The Russian and Polish troops were advancing towards Selicia. The snow lay deep. It was one of the cruellest winters, bitter cold and the snow was falling continuously. The exodus from the East had started, and continued day after day. The refugees came right through our town, along the Bahnhof Strasse, past our house to the station. Some were pulling carts or wheelbarrows loaded high with the few possessions they could take with them. Some were pushing prams loaded with bags and carrying the baby, all wrapped up warm. You could just see their eyes.

There were mothers with young children and old people. Many had only the clothes they were wearing. The convoys of refugees continued night and day. They were cold and exhausted. At the station they were given blankets and some soup, and put on trains. Where the trains were taking them, we didn't know, nor what happened to the carts and prams, which were left behind.

Every day Ingrid and I and many others helped the refugees. We went to the outskirts of Kanth and helped carry children or pull the carts. At the station it was utter chaos. Trains ran infrequently. Everywhere was packed with refugees, hoping to get another train. Many gave up waiting and carried on walking. We helped by making sandwiches and hot drinks. We felt so sorry for these people, not realising we would be refugees ourselves very soon. Why did Hitler start this terrible war?

One day a telegram arrived informing Martha that her

Chapter Three
The War Years 1939–1945

husband had been wounded. He was being transported to a Military Hospital.

Mutti and Martha were becoming very concerned. Hanna, our daily help, had been sent home to look after her elderly parents. We heard from some of the helpers that an elderly woman had died on the side of the road near one of the villages. A young woman gave birth in the snow. Both mother and baby froze to death.

Chapter Four
Leaving Kanth

It was a bitter cold morning again in early February 1945 when Mutti woke us up and told us, 'We are going to Dresden. It is too dangerous to stay any longer.' The Russian and Polish troops were advancing into Selicia at an alarming speed. We could hear heavy shelling and bombs exploding in the distance.

Mutti had made a small linen bag for each of us, which we wore on a belt under our clothing. That's where we carried our birth certificates, identity passports and some money. We made our way to the station, carrying some suitcases and my violin. Our most important possessions, like photos and papers, were in Mutti's bag.

We tried to persuade Martha to come with us with her two children, but she wouldn't hear of it. She insisted on staying behind. She was worried that Richard would not be able to find them if they left. She knew that he was wounded, but had no way of letting him know where she would be.

The station was packed with refugees; many were still arriving, all hoping for another train to take them to safety. We almost gave up hope, when suddenly a train reversed into the station. It didn't come from Breslau; maybe the lines or even the station in Breslau had been destroyed. There was a terrible scramble and pushing, everybody was desperate to get on the train. Soldiers appeared from somewhere and tried to bring order into the chaos.

I didn't know Mutti could be so pushy, but she did quite some elbowing herself and made sure we got onto the train. Just as I stepped up holding on to Mutti's coat, a soldier tapped me on the shoulder, grabbed my violin and said with a harsh voice, 'No fancy goods, hand luggage only.'

He took my violin. I was completely shocked and upset. The violin case wouldn't have taken up much room, but there was

Chapter Four
Leaving Kanth

nothing I could do. My violin was gone. We sat huddled together, at least we had made it onto the train. We waited and waited, but the train didn't leave for about three hours. Then, at last, it started to move very slowly. After a few miles we stopped again. All we could see, looking out of the windows, was snow, miles of snow, and some snow-covered rooftops in the distance. It looked pretty like a Christmas card.

It was the same all through the journey, slowly progressing for a few miles, then long periods of waiting in the middle of nowhere. Everything was white. It was really eerie, especially at night. When we stopped in a station, some Red Cross people passed mugs of coffee and sandwiches up to us. Now and again we managed to get some sleep on each other's shoulders. The journey to Dresden, which normally took just four hours, took four days and nights. We were exhausted, hungry and feeling very dirty. At last we had arrived in Dresden. From the station in Dresden-Neustadt, we took the tram to Oma's house. Oma had been very worried. We had no way of letting her know of our long delay. On the radio was no mention of the refugees' plight.

Two young lady friends from our hometown came to see us the next day. Johanna and Ilse were a few years older than I. They told us all about their journey hitch hiking back to Kanth the previous week. They had originally arrived in Dresden two weeks earlier and had gone back to Kanth to rescue some more belongings. They made it sound so easy and exciting to hitchhike. They planned to go again the next day and wanted me to join them.

Mutti and Oma would not hear of it at first, but after the girls assured them that the three of us would be alright, and promised to take extra care, I pleaded with Mutti to let me try and persuade Martha to come back with us. All I was hoping for was to get Martha out and back to Dresden with us. Finally they agreed to let me go.

Returning for Martha – 8th February 1945

Early in the morning we were ready to leave. With boots and warm clothing and some money in our body bags, we set off full of enthusiasm and hope. We took turns carrying the rucksack

Chapter Four
Leaving Kanth

with some food and drink. Not very much, as we were sure we could buy things on route.

We made our way down to the river Elbe and walked for a long while, 'till we came to a very large crossroads. We took the route towards Bautzen, a town about 80 km from Dresden. After a few hours walking, taking occasional short rests, we stopped in a small town called Radeberg. Sitting on the steps of a little church, we had a snack from the rucksack. Then we rested again for a while before continuing on our way. It was very cold.

Soon we were lucky to get a lift to the outskirts of Bautzen. It was snowing again and getting dark. In Bischofswalde we stayed in a small hostel for the night. Though it was full up with refugees, the owner let us stay in the lounge. I fell asleep on a chair, and when I nearly fell off, it woke me up with a start. It was still dark outside when we left.

We bypassed Bautzen and managed to get a lift to Goerlitz, where we had a meal in a small cafe. When we asked for the direction to Bunslau and Liegnitz, we got some strange looks. People were coming *from* the east, not going *to* the east.

It had taken two days and nights since leaving Dresden, to get as far as Jauer, a small town between Liegnitz and Striegau, sometimes getting lifts in military transports. Germany was in such chaos at the time, that soldiers were able to give civilians lifts in military vehicles. But a lot of the time we were walking, the snow crunching under our feet.

Everything seemed eerie. It was cold and dismal looking as we walked along country roads. All the time people were coming from the opposite direction, on horse-drawn carts, cars, bikes, with wheelbarrows or on foot. Women and children and old people, all weary and in a state of distress.

It was nighttime; we heard gunfire and explosions. In the distance we saw the black night sky illuminated with lights, Liegnitz was on fire. It was a frightening sight. Yet we were determent to carry on. All there was on my mind was getting to Kanth somehow and getting Martha and her children out, and back with us to Dresden.

German soldiers in tanks were passing us coming from the East, as we walked to the next village. Just in front of us two heavy

Chapter Four
Leaving Kanth

armoured Panzer Tanks were positioned in the middle of the road. A German soldier approached us and told us to go back. No way could we go any further, as the Russians had already taken over the next village.

Just then some women came running across the fields with their children. They had no possessions, only the clothes they were wearing. Some still had their pinafores on. They were panic-stricken and breathless. They too urged us to go back, 'The Russians are on our farms.'

Turning back to Dresden – 10th February 1942

Reluctantly we gave up and turned back. The journey back was most eventful. We walked, again, for miles. When we passed another farm, we saw in front of us a wagon loaded high with hay. The farmer, who was leading the horses, told us he was taking the hay from his barn to the animals in the field. We asked him if we could join him. He was very friendly. He stopped the horses and told us to climb up on to the hay. I don't know how I got up there, but I did. It was really comfortable on the hay and we soon fell asleep.

I don't know how long we slept. Suddenly we were woken up by the sound of planes and explosions. We slipped down from the wagon very fast, and helped the man to uncouple the horses. Then we all jumped into the ditch by the roadside.

While we were crouching in the ditch, we saw two planes circling overhead. We actually saw the bombs falling. They were Russian planes and they were aiming at the nearby station. It had all happened so suddenly, and seemed over again in minutes. When the planes were gone, we got up and decided to carry on walking. Luckily the farmer still had hold of the horses, but we said our 'thank you' and 'goodbye' and made our way.

Crossing the railway lines we saw the bomb craters on the railway lines. The station itself was only slightly damaged. When we were far enough away from the station, we wanted to rest and stop somewhere for the night. There was a petrol station, where we could have stopped perhaps, but we were now wary of the Russians attacking a petrol station. So we carried on walking.

My legs were heavy like lead. I even walked with my eyes

Chapter Four
Leaving Kanth

closed at times. We were now nearing the Riesengebirge (Giant Mountain Range). We cheered ourselves up by singing a funny German marching song. Here is the German version first:

> *Klotz, Klotz, Klotz am Bein. Klavier vorm Bauch,*
> *Wie lang ist die Schaussee?*
> *Rechts sind Baueme, links sind Baueme*
> *Und dazwischen Zwischenraueme.*
>
> *Was moegen das fuer Baueme sein,*
> *Wo die Grossen*
> *E-le-phanten spazieren geh'n*
> *Ohne sich zu stossen.*

I'll try and give you an equivalent English version, not a true translation though!

> Carrying a piano from around your neck,
> And pulling a log from your heels,
> But we're tough and determined, oh heck,
> So we walk, 'cause we haven't got no wheels.
>
> How far do you think this road will go,
> And where is it likely to end?
> We want to get all the way there, you know,
> We don't want to go round the bend.

We marched along merrily, singing our tune. It's amazing how that helped. Our legs didn't seem quite so heavy anymore.

Later that day we saw a couple of farmhands working in a field. I think they were collecting winter cabbage. Another worker was digging up the snowy field with a horse-drawn plough ready for next year. Behind the hedge we spotted a basket. Hidden by the bushes we crept up to the basket and had a look inside. There were a number of sandwiches, thick farm bread with fillings. We helped ourselves to a sandwich each. Thick ham sandwiches, they were absolutely delicious, especially as we were quite hungry. We left the men enough food, but those stolen sandwiches were the

Chapter Four
Leaving Kanth

best ones we ever tasted, I'm sure.

It was beginning to snow again. In the next town we bought some apples. When we asked the shopkeeper where we could stay the night, he told us that everywhere was occupied with refugees, but we were welcome to stay in his hallway 'till morning. We were very grateful and managed to get some sleep sitting on the floor with our backs to the wall. It's surprising in what uncomfortable positions you can sleep when you're tired.

Next morning we thanked the shopkeeper and continued our journey back to Dresden. Before we left he gave us some freshly baked rolls for the journey, for which he would not accept any money, nor ration cards.

After a few miles walking in the snow, we were wondering how much further it was to Hirschberg. We were hoping for another lift. The road rose sharply uphill. On the left of the roadside were the mountains and on the right was a sheer drop. All the snow-covered trees and houses in the distance were a beautiful sight.

The road seemed endless, but at last our luck changed. Slowly creeping up the hill a German tank approached. Not the heavy, armoured kind, but a smaller kind with caterpillar tracks over several wheels. (I hope I have explained it properly.) The driver slowed down just enough for us to climb into the moving vehicle.

It kept snowing. It was quite cold in the tank, being open. The driver introduced himself as Helmut. He was trying to rejoin his regiment. I don't know whether Helmut fell asleep, or the road was too slippery, but something was suddenly wrong. He shouted, 'I can't move the lever.' And just then the tank tipped over to the right and we rolled down into the ditch. If it had been a deep ravine or sheer drop, like in many places, I don't think I would be here to tell you about it.

We were shaken, but unharmed – only Ilse had a small gash in her forehead. We helped each other out of the upturned tank and climbed back up to the road. The four of us now slowly carried on walking. After some more miles on the mountain road, an Army lorry came slowly crawling up the hill. A couple of soldiers, sitting in the back, helped the four of us climb into the back of the lorry. No way could the driver have stopped, he would not have

Chapter Four
Leaving Kanth

been able to start again up the slippery hill. We got a lift as far as Zittau, where the tank driver left us to go his way.

On the crossroads in the direction of Bautz en, we stopped to decide what to do next. We all agreed that we needed a rest. We were tired, hungry and in need of a bath, but for the bath we knew we had to wait. We went to a roadside café. We had enough money between us to get some soup, but we had no ration cards left. The cafe was full of people, so we decided to walk on. Maybe we could rest somewhere else. Just as we stepped outside, a soldier tapped Ilse on the shoulder and said, 'I heard you talking; you're on your way to Dresden?'

He offered to give us a lift. He was on his way to Meissen. His articulated lorry was parked in the car park of the cafe. We were very glad of another lift and squeezed into the cab next to the driver. He told us his name was Fritz and that he was delivering the goods in the trailer to a garrison.

The progress through the mountains near Zittau was very slow, but at least it was warm in the cab. Fritz shared his sandwiches with us. We were singing to keep each other awake. Though it was nighttime, everything outside looked white. Under normal circumstances we would have enjoyed the beautiful scenery. The moon was shining and it had stopped snowing. In the distance we saw the dim lights of a town. It was Bautzen.

The road now was quite steep downhill and thick with snow. Fritz was driving very slowly in low gear, yet he had to apply the brakes very carefully all the time. The weight of the trailer caused the whole vehicle to slip. The trailer skidded sideways, and no matter how hard Fritz tried to keep the lorry on the road, it kept skidding, and the trailer went off the road, hanging over the cliff, and our cab came to a stop on the edge of the road. It was a terrifying experience, the seconds ticked away. Fritz told us to sit absolutely still, while he carefully climbed out of the cab and uncoupled the trailer. It went crashing down the cliff. Silently I thanked our Guardian Angel that the cab didn't follow the trailer. Fritz told us that the trailer was loaded with cigarettes and tobacco, but whether that was true, I don't know. We drove away from the edge and into town. After a short break, Fritz offered to take us all the way to Dresden.

The Albert Bruecke over the River Elbe.

Chapter Four
Leaving Kanth

The rest of the journey was uneventful. We were just grateful that we were on our way home to Oma's. We arrived near the station in Dresden-Neustadt in the early afternoon of the 13th February 1945. We said goodbye to Fritz and walked the rest of the way to Glacis-Strasse, Oma's house.

Mutti, Oma and Ingrid had been very worried. They were so relieved to see us back, though without Martha. I kept thinking about Martha, about our home and all my friends. Would we ever be able to go back home again? Though I was very tired, I had a quick bath. Oma gave me a bowl of soup, but I slumped onto the settee and fell asleep. I had a couple of hours sleep, when Mutti woke me up and gave me the option of joining them on a visit to my Godmother Auntie Charlotte and her mother.

Chapter Five
The Night of 13–14 February 1945

Aunt Charlotte and her Mum lived in Dresden-Altstadt. The bridge which led over the river Elbe to the Old Town was the Albert Bruecke. We took the tram from Glacis Strasse over the bridge. There were some boats on the river. It all looked so peaceful. I admired the ornamental carvings on the sides of the buildings we passed.

Auntie Charlotte was, as usual, very pleased to see us and wanted to know all about my journey, hitchhiking back to Selicia. After coffee and cake and a lot of chatter, I almost fell asleep again. We left at about seven o'clock. When we said 'goodbye' we had no idea we would never see them again.

Back at Oma's house, I relaxed on the sofa and fell asleep. At 10 p.m. Mutti shook me awake. The air-raid sirens were sounding and then we heard bombs exploding. We hurried down to the cellar. The other residents were also on their way down. The cellar was not a proper bomb shelter. It was just used for storage. Nobody expected Dresden to be bombed. We heard later that Hitler had been given an ultimatum; to capitulate or Dresden would be blown to pieces. None of the politicians warned the people, but they themselves made sure they were in a safe place.

It was arranged by the British Air Ministry that targets such as Berlin, Chemists, Leipzig and Dresden should prove to be vital in destroying communication, and the evacuation from East Germany, Breslau being another main objective. 'Heavy air attacks will cause great confusion in civilian evacuation from the East.' Later the bombing of Dresden received much criticism worldwide.

In the cellar we sat on some boxes among the bikes and coal etc. and listened to the sound of the explosions. It was very frightening. After about twenty minutes all seemed quiet again.

Chapter Five
The Night of 13–14 February 1945

Then we heard the 'All Clear' siren.

When we left the cellar we smelled burning. A bomb had hit our roof and the top floor was on fire. All the residents passed buckets of water up the stairs to each other, and eventually the fire was extinguished.

Back in Oma' s flat on the second floor, we talked for a long while about this terrible war, which nobody wanted or could understand. Mutti got some bags and cases packed with the most important possessions, like photos, jewellery and valuable mementos. Just in case.

None of us felt like going to bed. We were just talking about the happenings of the last few years and this dreadful war. I didn't seem to feel tired anymore.

Saint Valentines Day – 14th February 1945

The sirens sounded again at 1 a.m. I just had time to put my slippers on, when we heard the first bombs exploding. We all grabbed what we could and hurried down to the cellar. Hearing the explosions, and even the whistling of the bombs falling, was very frightening. At one stage we heard the whistling and a loud explosion, and the whole house seemed to shake. I had the awful feeling that our house had been hit. Silently we just sat there, saying a prayer, waiting. This time the bombing lasted for about half an hour.

It seemed ages before we realised everything had gone quiet. For a few minutes the silence was eerie. Cautiously we left the cellar. The hallway and the stairs were pitch black and full of smoke. We could smell burning. The other residents joined us in the hallway, and among our whispers we heard the crackling of the fire. It was useless trying to go upstairs; there was thick smoke and rubble on the stairs. It made us cough. We had no option but to try and leave the building.

Oma went to the back yard and fetched a wheelbarrow from one of the sheds, in which we put our few cases and bags. The safest place at the time was the big car showroom across the main road. All the huge showroom windows were smashed, the cars were a mess, but at least it wasn't burning in that building. We could still hear explosions in the distance, but we didn't know if

Dresden recalls the Night of the Devil's Tinderbox

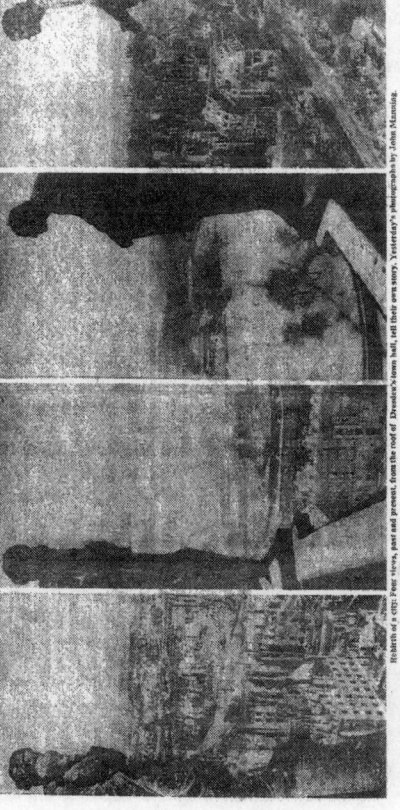

Rebirth of a city: Four views, past and present, from the roof of Dresden's town hall, tell their own story. Yesterday's photographs by John Manning

From Alan Hamilton
Dresden

Forty years ago tonight at ten minutes past ten, the RAF-led air raid sirens wailed across the rooftops of Dresden, a baroque city in southern Europe.

Dresden had always thought itself safe. But it was a strategic rail and industrial centre, and the city had no proper air-raid shelter; its inhabitants had not evacuated.

Such a treasure trove of art and architecture, its population of 630,000 was swelled by half a million refugees fleeing before the advance of the Red Army, said the east.

The city, known as the jewel of Saxony, had been pounded and burnt to rubble by the most devastating

and since, say the most unnecessary air raid of the pre-atomic age. Eight hundred RAF bombers, plus American aircraft the next day, dropped incendiary and high-explosive bombs on the these inner-incorporated or suburban areas. That night an estimated 135,000 German civilians perished.

In this season of 40th anniversaries of the last European war, the destruction of Dresden will be marked today by a small group of British visitors, led by the Lord Mayor of Coventry, a city with which Dresden has been twinned since 1956. There will be a simple ceremony of prayer and wreath-laying and a performance

of the Dresden Requiem by the Irish composer Cormac O'Duffy, last heard in Coventry Cathedral in 1985.

One of the wreaths will be laid by men who took part as bomber crews, who said yesterday they were merely "seeing the flames of their night's work over 500 miles away".

Clergy and volunteers from Coventry have travelled to Dresden regularly since 1965 and have helped to rebuild a wing of the damaged Diakonissen Hospital, whose chapel contains a cross made with nails that fell from the roof of Coventry Cathedral on the night of its inferno in 1940. The dean of Coventry, the Very Rev J.H. Petty, was a pilot shot down over the carriage of Dresden.

The Rt Rev John Gibbs, Bishop of Coventry, who will take part in a joint British-German ceremony today said: "We are here in peace and reconciliation, with no political message."

The East Germans, now masters of Dresden, see a bigger event, following the Soviet principle of using the occasion to rage against the crimes of Hitlerite fascism. That Dresden was as great a British request is unlikely to be raised.

Herr Erich Honecker, the East German Communist Party leader, will address a major rally in the city square, and, in the evening, Dresden's magnificent fifty-year-old opera

house, whose painstaking reconstruction has just been completed, will stage a gala performance of Weber's Der Freischütz, the last opera to be performed there before the bombs impacted four decades of silence.

Councillor Walter Brandfels, Lord Mayor of Coventry, and his party, except the British Ambassador to East Berlin, will be among the audience in the specially rebuilt theatre auditorium.

Of the British party... was a radar operator... fires of hell than Mrs Erica Woodham, now living in London and married to an Englishman. The 55-year-old meets

year-old German girl cowering in a cellar as the firestorm fed the flames like bellows on a furnace. She later studied the very sandstone of the city... the masonry, crashed onto its own foundations. She was saved by an air raid warden who led her through a warren of cellars to safety by the waters of the River Elbe.

Mrs Erica... later brought... with other survivors.

"So many memories died, it was as hard to live these conversations. I would meet like ne... met in Dresden on ... today."

Altmarkt – Wochenlang wurden Tote gestapelt und verbrannt

Chapter Five
The Night of 13–14 February 1945

those were bombs or gas mains blowing up. I can't remember hearing the 'All Clear' siren – maybe that place had also been destroyed.

Standing among the broken glass and wrecked cars, watching Oma's beautiful house burn down, was an awful sight. The biggest flames came out of the windows on the second floor, Oma's apartment.

We were told later, that an estimated 136,000 people had been killed in that one night. Thousands of refugees had come to Dresden. The stations were packed with refugees at the time. Dresden-Altstadt was almost completely destroyed. We lost our Godmother, Auntie Charlotte, her mother and my other Godmother Auntie Erna, who lived in Dresden-Radebeul.

Later, parts of the Altstadt had to be burned out with flame-throwers, to prevent diseases spreading. It would have been an impossible task to dig out all the dead, and to bury them. The Circus Sarasani had been hit, and many of the animals got killed. Dresden was so beautiful; there were no military objectives in this capital, only works of art and a military hospital. Everything was completely or partially destroyed – historical churches, art galleries, museums, the Opera House and the huge beautiful castle right by the river Elbe. The *Zwinger* (Wall Pavilion) was also destroyed. Thousands of innocent people died. War is a terrible thing, every country suffered. The people don't want it, yet terrible atrocities were committed on both sides. None of the German people wanted Hitler to go to war, and none of us had a chance to stop him.

Leaving the Ruins

It was still nighttime, or rather the early hours of the morning. The sky was a strange looking smoky colour, lit up by all the fires. When we were sure we couldn't hear any more explosions, we left the wrecked car showroom, the broken glass crunching under our feet. I was only wearing slippers and had to be extra careful. The air smelled smoky. We had to dodge burning timber and soot flying about in the breeze, as we made our way down to the river Elbe. Ingrid and I pulled the wheelbarrow with our few possessions.

Chapter Five
The Night of 13–14 February 1945

We stopped at one of Oma's friends' house, which didn't seem too badly damaged, only the windows were missing. We could only see the front of her house, she told us the back was badly damaged. Other bomb victims already occupied her house. She offered us coffee before we made our way again. We had no idea where to go. All we wanted was to get out of Dresden, but where to?

The Albert Bruecke was damaged. One of the boats on the river was still ablaze. The Red Cross put up a soup kitchen on the side of the road. We had a much appreciated potato soup. Many people joined us, all survivors of the bombing. Nobody knew where to go. We were all walking in the middle of the road. There was no traffic; no trams were in operation. The houses and churches we passed were in ruin. They were still smouldering. There was not a single building undamaged as far as the eye could see.

At 3 o'clock that afternoon Dresden was under attack again. By then we were on the road along the river, and managed to hide in the doorway of a derelict church. Again, we listened to bombs exploding. Thankfully it was over quite soon. We carried on walking.

Suddenly a plane flew low over us, and with a machine gun fired into the middle of the road. We all ran to the sides and tried to hide somewhere, but it was all over in minutes. I don't know, if the pilot meant to kill anybody, or if he just had fun scattering the people.

How long we carried on walking for I am not sure, but for Oma's sake we had to take a rest. Oma, though, had other ideas. She wanted to go as far as Pirna, where some more of her friends lived.

It was getting dark and we were exhausted, so we had to find somewhere to stay the night. We stopped at a church, and as we went through the gate, we realized there were already a number of refugees there, trying to find shelter. Though the church was damaged, the inner door was locked. We stayed in the entrance vestibule.

Putting the wheelbarrow in the corner, we huddled together along the wall to keep each other warm. Eventually we fell asleep

The Chrurch where my parents got married (Before and after 14th February 1945

Chapter Five
The Night of 13–14 February 1945

for a while. In the morning we were on our way again. By now we were very hungry. Oma tried to buy some rolls and cheese in a grocer's shop, but the shops were closed.

At last we got to Pima. Oma's friend's house was on the outskirts of the town, a pretty little house with a lovely front garden. We waited with the wheelbarrow by the gate, while Oma went to the door. The two ladies were pleased to see each other, but we couldn't stay there. The house was already full up with refugees. Oma came back to the gate very sad looking. I just burst into tears. The happenings of the last few days got to me. What, if I hadn't got back to Dresden on the day of the bombing? If I had been too late, I might never have seen my family again. Why did we lose everything, first in Selicia, and now in Dresden? I felt so sorry for Oma and Mutti, having no home and nowhere to go. So I pulled myself together, my tears wouldn't help them, I told myself.

As we were walking away, Oma' s friend came rushing out. She asked us to stay the night in her kitchen. Every room, even the hallway was occupied. She gave Mutti and Oma a blanket and they found room on the floor in the hallway with some other people. Ingrid and I slept under the kitchen table.

Next morning we left Pima. We were trying to make our way to Obersdorf in Bavaria. It was there that my parents had arranged we should meet, should anything happen. Hopefully Vati would either be there or get in touch with Auntie Trudie, who owned a guesthouse in Obersdorf.

After a couple of days on the road, resting and sleeping in doorways of ruins, we reached a Red Cross Meeting Point, where all the refugees were given help and advice. We were told to wait for a specially arranged train, which would take us to a refugee camp in Southern Germany. Someone advised us to buy some bread and drink, as it was unclear for how long we would be travelling.

When the train pulled into the station, it was a cattle wagon with eight or ten carriages. The floors were covered with straw. We were told to climb in, but nobody could tell us where we were going. We had to leave our wheelbarrow behind, but were able to take our hand luggage. Everybody made themselves as comfortable

Chapter Five
The Night of 13–14 February 1945

as possible on the straw, old men, women and children.

It wasn't too long before the train started to move slowly. The sliding doors of the wagons were slightly ajar, with a chain across leaving about a foot wide opening. There were a few small shutters at the sides. It was quite dark inside. How many people were in our wagon I'm not sure. We heard a baby crying and an old man had quite a nasty cough.

The train often stopped for several hours, in what seemed like 'No-man's Land'. All we could see through the gap in the door was snow. I wondered where the toilets were. There were none. If you were desperate you had to climb out, when the train was stationary, and hide somewhere in the snow, hoping the train wouldn't move, while you were indisposed.

Occasionally we drove slowly through small stations, which were deserted in the middle of the night. The names were completely unfamiliar. When we stopped in one of the stations for a few hours we had a chance to use the toilets and also have a quick wash. We realized we were in Czechoslovakia.

The nights were terribly cold. During the day, when the sun was shining for a while, the snow on the carriage roofs melted and dripped on us. Often the train stopped for hours. Then we were glad to be able to stretch our legs, as long as we didn't move too far from the train.

The straw was wet and uncomfortable. We were hungry and cold. Nobody knew where we were going. After several days we reached a big station. I felt that we were at last back to civilisation. The bustle and activity on the platform was really comforting. The town was Prague. Red Cross ladies came along the train with trolleys and gave everybody enamel mugs with soup, or coffee, and sandwiches.

All together we travelled for ten days and nights. At last we stopped and were told to get off the train. We had reached our destination. Lorries were waiting outside the small station. The refugees were allocated different lorries, to be taken to different villages. We were somewhere in the south of Austria, on the border of Czechoslovakia.

Oma, Mutti, Ingrid and I were taken to a little village called Jarmirn with about twenty other refugees. Old and young, men,

Chapter Five
The Night of 13–14 February 1945

women and children were housed together in one big classroom in the village school. All over the floor, along the walls of the classroom were straw mattresses. We put our coats over those for more comfort. We were so grateful, to be able to stay somewhere for a while, and above all, to be alive.

Jarmirn, Spring 1945

The people in this village were very friendly and helpful. Soon Mutti found us rooms with a miller's family. Mutti, Ingrid and I shared a room, and Oma had one to herself. The rooms were clean, though very basic. Some of the other refugees also found themselves private accommodation.

The *Buergermeister* (Mayor) of Jarmirn issued everybody with new ration cards. Without them you couldn't buy any food, but with them it was sometimes not possible to get what you were entitled to, because transportation and supply just wasn't organised anymore towards the end of the war – the whole economy was in complete chaos. We lived mainly on eggs, of which the farmers gave us plenty.

By now the weather had improved considerably, it had stopped snowing and it was getting warmer. It was almost springtime.

One day, Mutti, Ingrid and I and the miller's daughter walked to the next town. We had almost forgotten that there was a war on. We were walking along the country road, when suddenly an airplane appeared. It flew very low over us. We jumped into the ditch, just as the middle of the road was sprayed with machine gun fire. We stayed in the ditch quite shaken. The plane, one of a small convoy we saw in the distance, circled a couple of times and then left. It was a Russian plane, the pilot must have realised four females wasn't a worthwhile target. We abandoned the intention to go to the next town and made our way back to Jarmirn.

Mutti got very depressed, she often cried. She was not only worried about our predicament, but especially about Vati. Where was Vati? Had he been in touch with Auntie Trudie yet? We tried to get transport to Obersdorf, but there were no trains or other means of transport. We had to wait.

One morning the *Buergermeister* personally brought Mutti a

Chapter Five
The Night of 13–14 February 1945

letter. After he had left, Mutti explained the context of the letter. I was called up! Any youth from the age of fourteen was to join the army. I was to report to the nearest garrison, a place just outside of Gmuend, and bring my own boots, blanket and *weapon*. Of all things they expected me to have a *weapon*! I didn't even have boots or a blanket. We were absolutely shocked. We had heard that boys as young as fourteen had been called up, but girls?

Mutti was in a real dilemma. As Ingrid had tonsillitis at that time, Mutti sent the form back, with a certificate from the local doctor (who put my name instead of Ingrid's on the certificate) stating that I had tonsillitis. That same day we packed our few possessions together and very early the next morning we left Jarmirn. The miller's wife gave us another tray of eggs to take with us.

We walked to the next crossroads, hoping and praying for a vehicle to give us a lift. Luck was on our side. An Army Jeep stopped and the driver agreed to take us as far as Linz. As we climbed into the jeep, Mutti accidentally sat on the tray of eggs. Luckily not many were broken, but the ones that were, made an awful mess on Mutti's posterior. We cleaned Mutti's coat with lots of tissues as best we could. It was nice to have something to laugh about.

> 'There were two dozen eggs on that tray,
> How many survived, I can't say.
> They'd been sadly forgotten,
> When my dear mother's bottom
> Sat on the beggars that day.'

In Linz, Oma was able to obtain a small handcart, on which we loaded our luggage. We walked to the other end of town, to the crossroads. People were giving us some strange looks. Four females looking dishevelled and dusty, pulling a handcart right through the middle of town? I wonder what they thought? We saw the beautiful Donau (the river Danube). Slowly we carried on walking, hoping to get transport to Salzburg, another lovely town in Austria. We hadn't walked very far, when we saw an empty Army lorry and two officers standing nearby.

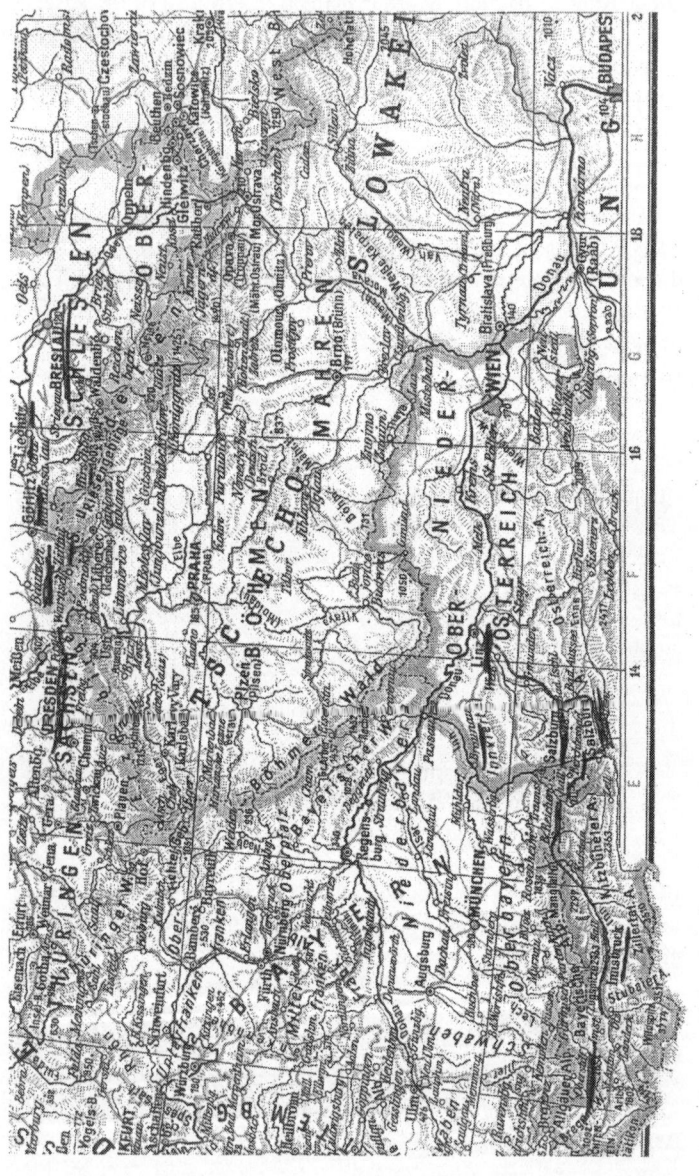

Chapter Five
The Night of 13–14 February 1945

Mutti approached them and asked where they were going and if they could possibly give us a lift. They were very friendly and told us they were on their way to Wegscheid and would gladly give us a lift. They assured us that near Wegscheid was a Red Cross Centre, where we could get further assistance.

The two officers lifted the handcart with our entire luggage on to the lorry and gave us all a 'push-up'. When we arrived in Wegscheid, we couldn't find the Red Cross Centre. As we had enough on our ration cards we decided to go to a cafe for a hot meal, and had a rather watery vegetable soup with meatballs.

Later we found the road in the direction of Salzburg. There was another family already waiting there. They had an enormous amount of luggage. They would need an empty lorry to themselves. We got chatting to them; they had also lost their home and were trying to go to Muenchen (Munich), where they had relations. I hope they didn't have to wait too long for transport, but we were, once more, very lucky. After a short wait an articulated lorry stopped, the trailer was full of gas canisters. The driver said he was on his way to Salzburg. He shifted some of the canisters to make room for the handcart. Mutti and Oma sat in the cab with the driver, while Ingrid and I sat in the back on the canisters.

It was not a very comfortable journey. We travelled all night. On one occasion we had to stop because of an air attack nearby. Though we had been travelling with dipped lights, the driver quickly switched the lights off and we climbed down and waited on the side of the road. We saw flashing lights in the distance, probably minor explosions. After some time we were able to continue our journey.

In Salzburg we stopped right outside a bakery. Oma was able to buy some bread and a little cheese for our breakfast. The ration cards had to last us 'till we got to Obersdorf.

Soon we were again lucky and managed to persuade a potato merchant to give us a lift to the next town. He told us we would find a Red Cross Centre there, but unfortunately it was shut. We realised we were in Berchtesgaden. What a beautiful town, and what a wonderful view from just outside on the mountain road overlooking the valley. How I would have loved to spend some

Chapter Five
The Night of 13–14 February 1945

time there in peacetime.

We waited on the outskirts of Berchtesgaden nearly all morning, too tired to carry on walking, when a German soldier joined us. He had been on compassionate leave, in Dresden, where he also lost everything, and his only surviving relatives lived in Italy. He was, like us, trying to get transport to Innsbruck and from there continue to Italy. We were pleased of his company and it was easier for a soldier to hail a vehicle.

The sirens sounded in town, but there was nothing we could do, there was nowhere to go, only the trees for shelter. Soon a van stopped. That only went as far as Lofer, where the driver had to turn off towards Zell-am-See. He gave us a lift to Lofer. Here we were hoping to continue our journey and get connection to Innsbruck.

Lofer, April 1945

On arrival in Lofer, a pretty little town surrounded by mountains, we first of all went to a cafe with our escort, the German soldier, and had coffee and rolls. Later, on the way to the other end of town, we saw an LKW – an articulated lorry – parked outside the hotel Zum Schweitzer. The driver, who introduced himself as Corporal Koehler, told us that he was on his way to Bludenz. Unfortunately his lorry had broken down and he was waiting for the spare parts he needed, before he could leave, probably in a couple of days.

We were very relieved at the prospect of another lift and didn't mind waiting another two days. The hotel Zum Schweitzer was fully occupied by refugees, but we were able to stay the night on some benches in the barn, next to the servants' quarters When, after two days, the lorry still wasn't repaired, we managed to get two rooms on the third floor of the hotel. Oma and Mutti shared one room, while Ingrid and I had the other one.

After ten days the lorry was still not repaired. We heard that once it was again roadworthy, it was to be confiscated by the army to bring supplies to the area. This was very upsetting news for us.

One night, well past midnight, we were woken by a loud commotion in the corridors. Hotel staff were knocking on all the doors and asking the guests to vacate their rooms immediately.

View of Lofer and mountains

Mutti

Lofer Highstreet and bakery

Chapter Five
The Night of 13–14 February 1945

Gestapo officers had arrived in the area and were demanding the hotel for themselves and their girlfriends.

We all had to get out in the middle of the night. Once again we were in the street, not knowing where to go. Some of the refugees were given shelter in the farmhouse, while others managed to find accommodation privately the next day. We stayed again in the barn on some benches until morning. Next day we were able to get a room in the hotel Zur Post.

One day Mutti was talking to the owner of the post office. He advised Mutti not to try and travel on to Bavaria. It would be safer to stay in Lofer for the time being. The French army was already near the Algaue (Bavaria). No way would we get as far as Obersdorf. It would be best to wait and see. We had no option but to stay. Mutti was very sad. We were all worried about Vati. *When will this war be over? When will we find Vati? Surely things must improve eventually, when this terrible war is over…*

Chapter Six
The End of the War

Hitler and Gobbels died in Berlin. The Russians occupied Berlin. On the 8th May 1945, the 'Total Capitulation of Germany' was signed in Reims by Keitel and Jodel. Gross admiral Doenitz took over the leadership of Germany in the last few days after Hitler's death.

On both sides of Lofer the American Army approached, from Innsbruck and from Salzburg. On the 8th May was the official end of the war. On that very day the Americans arrived in Lofer at 12 noon. This dreadful war was over at last!

We were very apprehensive at first. How were they going to treat us Germans? Ingrid and I were on the balcony watching. We crouched down and looked through the bars. The soldiers seemed very friendly. We saw them handing out chocolates to the children, who stood in doorways.

On Thursday 10th May 1945, the rest of the American occupation troops arrived in Lofer; altogether 480 men, we were told. They were billeted in the hotel Zum Schweitzer and other guesthouses.

We always looked for notification on the official notice board in the post office for any important news regarding the refugees. One order from the American Commandant was, that no civilians were allowed on the streets between 9 p.m. and 5.30 a.m. The swimming baths, which had been reopened since the American Occupation, were out of bounds for the German public between 1 and 4 in the afternoon, during which time it was solely for the use of the Army.

The food situation was still bad, even with ration cards you couldn't get half of what you were entitled to. There were no potatoes, no vegetables or fruit, and very little meat. There were no deliveries to the shops. At the bakery you had to queue up for

Chapter Six
The End of the War

ages first thing in the morning to be able to get a small loaf, or half a loaf, which was your weekly ration. Everybody had to buy their own bread; you couldn't get someone else's as well. Even Oma had to go and queue up to buy her own bread. At 5.30 a.m., as soon as curfew was lifted, we went to the bakery. There was always an endless queue.

In the hotel, where we stayed, we usually had for dinner a very watery soup, sometimes with a little rice in it, sometimes a few noodles. That was also taken from our ration cards. We were always hungry. The Americans, who occupied the hotel Zum Schweitzer (what happened to the Gestapo I don't know), sometimes threw cigarettes or chocolate from their balcony. People were very grateful. I remember seeing soldiers lounging about on their balconies, sitting on deck chairs and with their boots on the tables, giving wolf-whistles to girls passing by. I thought it rather funny and we appreciated being treated in this friendly way, and without hostility.

We had a lot to be grateful to Oma for. She was very adventurous. Every morning and evening she went to one of the American kitchens. They always gave her some food to take home, which was left over after the soldiers had been served. Nearly always she came back with a container of coffee and some porridge, sometimes some ham omelette. Occasionally she got some delicious tomato soup. It was never very much, but it all helped. Ingrid was able to go to school in the local camp, but History and Geography lessons were not being taught. These subjects were forbidden.

Friday, 25th May 1945

All prisoners of war (that must have included the Gestapo officers) had been moved to some other part of Germany. All non-residents of Lofer were eventually to be evacuated. That was good news for us. Going back to Selicia was out of the question. We were hoping at last to be able to go to Obersdorf to find Vati. But it still took several weeks.

In the meantime we made the best of our situation. Food was still very scarce. The Americans had stopped giving any food to the civilians. Nearly every day Ingrid and I went into the nearby

Chapter Six
The End of the War

woods picking blueberries, and later wild strawberries and wild mushrooms. *Steinpilze* and *Pfifferlinge* are my favourite mushrooms. They are absolutely delicious. Occasionally everybody got an extra ration of cheese.

It was in Lofer that I tasted my first (and last) horsemeat and cow's udder, which was on special offer, but you still had to queue up for it. The horsemeat was fried like steak. It was a bit tough and tasted somewhat sweet, as far as I can remember. The cow's udder was also fried in slices, coated with breadcrumbs, if you had any, and fried like steak. It was all soft and horrible inside. Yuck. We couldn't really allow ourselves to be fussy where food was concerned. I think I would even have appreciated spinach.

Although we wrote to Aunt Trudie, we had no idea whether she would receive our letters. We weren't even sure, if the Postal Service was in operation.

I made friends with an American soldier, Joe Collins. He came from Pittsburgh in Pennsylvania. He was very nice, well educated and polite. Mutti liked him too. Often Mutti came with us for walks in the mountains, and wild mushrooms and strawberry picking. When we went right to the top of one of the mountains, we had a wonderful view of Lofer and the whole valley. Joe told Mutti that he wished that one day I could come to America.

Ingrid and another girl managed to get a job in the American canteen for a while to serve meals and clear tables. She quite enjoyed this job, especially as she got good meals while on duty. Sometimes she was able to bring food home, like omelettes or creamy semolina pudding with sultanas. To this day Ingrid hates sultanas, but we were pleased she brought it home.

We leave Lofer

It was announced that all non-residents of Austria were to be evacuated from Lofer. The people who wanted to go to Bavaria were the first to go.

On the 25th July 1945, at 6.30 in the morning we were to meet at the marketplace, where a special transport was laid on to take us to Saalfelden. From there we were hoping to get a train to Augsburg or Munich. After further delays we finally arrived in

Chapter Six
The End of the War

Augsburg, where we hoped it would be easier to get a train to Obersdorf than it would have been from Munich. Unfortunately there were no trains running yet to Obersdorf. Again, we had to rely on other means of transport. We were very lucky and were able to spend the night in a hospital near the station. We also got a warm meal.

The next morning Oma spoke to a man as he came out of a shop to get to his car. He told us he was on his way to Sonthofen. Oma persuaded him to give us a lift. The handcart had already fallen to pieces by then. The man helped us put our few pieces of luggage in the boot. Then we drove off, through Kempten, arriving in Sonthofen before noon.

The next train didn't leave 'till 7.30 p.m. At last we arrived in Obersdorf. We left our luggage at the station and walked to the *Staufen* (the hill) where Aunt Trudie's guesthouse was, called 'Berghaus am Staufen'. It took us nearly an hour, slowly walking up the hill. Aunt Trudie was so glad to see us, but Vati was not there, and there had been no word from him. We were most relieved that we were made so welcome, Aunt Trudie wanted us to stay as long as we wanted to. Our first priority was to get registered in town and get ration cards.

To receive ration cards Ingrid and I had to prove that we were in employment. How our lives had changed dramatically in the past eight months or so. No more school, no more education, we had to get a job – any kind of job.

Ingrid was very lucky really. She got a job with a young mother, helping to look after her two-month-old baby boy. Ingrid worked from 8.30 in the morning 'till 1.30 in the afternoon. She liked her job very much.

I got a job in a cafe. Every morning I had to be there (in town) at 7 o'clock. The first thing I had to do was take the wheelbarrow and go to the local brewery. There a chap handed me huge blocks of ice down from the ramp. I put the ice blocks in the wheelbarrow, eight or ten in all. Back at the cafe I had to chop the ice up with a hammer into small pieces and put those into the back of the cold cabinet. We had no electric freezer. I felt absolutely frozen and my arms were aching.

After that, a large stone container was waiting for me in the

Chapter Six
The End of the War

backyard filled with potatoes. I had to scrub them in cold water, as there was no such luxury as warm water. My next task was peeling mountains of carrots and onions.

It didn't take very long before I developed a kidney and bladder infection. For several weeks I recuperated at Aunt Trudie's. When I recovered, Mutti didn't want me to go back to that cafe. I got a job with a farmer's family. It was a live-in job. The people were very nice, but the work was hard.

I had a small room to myself. Every morning I had to get up at 5 a.m. My first task was to clean out the huge kitchen range from the day before and light a fire with rolled up newspaper, twigs and logs. Then I had to wash a large saucepan full of potatoes and put them on to boil. Pouring the boiling water from the heavy saucepan was always a dreaded task. While the potatoes were boiling, I cleaned eight pairs of boots, which were neatly lined up by the back door every morning. Believe me, they were muddy.

For breakfast every other morning we had jacket potatoes with cottage cheese, and the alternate mornings I had to cook porridge, again a large saucepan full. There was a big wooden table in the middle of the kitchen with wooden benches, where we all sat for our meals – the parents, three children, the grandmother, two farm hands and myself. With the pot of potatoes and the dish of cottage cheese in the middle of the table, everybody helped themselves to what they wanted. The farm hands usually piled their plates up high. The same thing happened at all mealtimes – pots and dishes were put in the centre of the table and everybody just dug in with their own spoons or knives.

After breakfast I had to wash and dress the two youngest children and take them to kindergarten. Then the real housework began: dusting, cleaning, scrubbing, washing and making or changing beds. On Sunday mornings I had to go to church with the family. I would rather have stayed at home. Quite often I fell asleep during the service.

One Sunday evening I wanted to go to a local dance and asked permission to have the evening off. Reluctantly that was finally granted. I was very excited. I got ready in my best dress before the evening meal. When my work was done and it was time for me to go, I was in such a rush to get to the dance hall, that I realised to

Chapter Six
The End of the War

my horror and embarrassment after removing my coat, that I had forgotten to take my huge dark pinafore off. I tore it off quickly, screwed it up and hid it behind the coats, hoping that nobody had noticed.

After a few weeks working with the farmer's family, my kidney trouble started up again. I went back to Aunt Trudie's and was quite ill for a couple of weeks. Mutti wanted me to get more suitable employment. As I was always very interested in any form of art, she thought it might be helpful to take some of my sketches and drawings to the local Employment Agency. They were very helpful. I was allocated a job in a Pottery as an apprentice in Altstaedten, Sonthofen.

Every morning I had to catch the train at 6.30 and walk the short distance to the Pottery, arriving there about 7 o'clock before the rest of the staff arrived at 8 a.m. I had to light the fire under the kiln. Then I was able to practice on the pottery table. That was great fun.

It was a large room with five pottery tables, and worktops, which were used for painting the finished earthenware. On one side of the room were containers filled with the glaze for the finished articles.

I enjoyed this job very much. We all got on well. One young man, Franz, was a great dancer. When our boss wasn't in, he used to tap dance from pottery table to table, before they were in use and wet. He was an excellent dancer and we all enjoyed his performances.

I learned to make vases, jugs, bowls and all kind of articles. Sitting on a stool I pushed the heavy wheel with my right foot to rotate the turntable. With wet hands I put the clay onto the middle and attempted to form shapes. Well, what a wobbly mess it was at first, until I got the hang of it. I had a good and patient teacher, my boss.

After some weeks I was 'promoted' to paint the earthenware. I sat at one of the worktops, and placed the article to be painted with a gold rim onto a small, rotating tabletop. With steady hand I just held the brush to the rim and the moving tabletop did the rest. I also painted flowers, peacocks and other designs on vases and other crockery. I was in my element.

Chapter Six
The End of the War

Winter in Bavaria

For some time now, Ingrid and I were having riding lessons, though not together. I went on Saturday mornings. I loved horse riding and was looking forward to riding out into the countryside, but so far we had not ventured from the indoor arena. We also learnt to groom and saddle our horses.

There were eight pupils in my class. One day we were all lined up in the middle of the arena. The instructor was going to test us individually. We had to do trot, gallop, stop sharply, canter and ride the figure of eight. When it was my turn the instructor called, 'Timber!' – my horse's name. I must have been dreaming or maybe I had forgotten my horse's name, but as I didn't respond, my instructor hit Timber with his whip. Immediately Timber bolted and charged around the arena, throwing me against the wall and I landed on the floor. When I brushed the sawdust off my face, I realized I was lying between the horse's hind legs. Timber must have stopped instantly when I fell. I got back on and did the test. To ease my embarrassment I was told, 'You're not a fully-fledged rider until you have fallen off.'

At last we were told that we would be riding out into the countryside. We were all very eager and saddled our horses. The instructor led the way. Snow was lying on the ground, but the horses were used to that. When we passed a farm, a tractor was in front of the gate, switched on and making a horrible racket. The horses shied at the noise. The young boy riding in front of me slipped off his horse and refused to get back on. Our instructor told me to take the reins of the boy's horse and told him to go back to the stables. We somehow managed to ride past the tractor. Because the boy's horse was pulling one way, Timber suddenly decided to jump the fence. I fell off and landed head first in the snow. That must have been a funny sight, my legs poking out from the snow. Immediately I got up, brushed the snow off my face and arms and got back on the horse. This time I rode through an open gate, avoiding another jump over a fence.

After that incident I had free riding lessons in exchange for being interpreter in the classes for the American soldiers. That's how I met Harold Lewes, a very nice American soldier. We became good friends and he often came to visit us at Aunt

Chapter Six
The End of the War

Trudie's guesthouse.

Harold told us all about his life before he had to join the army, about his interesting profession. He was a technician and camera operator in Hollywood. He told us about some of the famous film stars he knew.

Sometimes we went for strolls in the mountains. To get to the Nebelhorn, a very high mountain in the Bavarian Alps, we went by cable car. Many people came up there in the cable car with their skis. It must have been great fun for them to ski back down again. Memories came flooding back, of when Ingrid and I used to go skiing at home in Selicia. There were no high mountains, but roads sloping down, and crossing the fields outside Kanth.

Harold saw me dreaming. So I told him a little about my life before this war started. We had coffee in the restaurant. It was a fantastic view from the top of the Nebelhorn. Eventually we made our descent by cable car.

Christmas 1945

One Saturday morning just before Christmas I was on my way into town to the riding school. As I have already described, winter in Bavaria is very cold and crisp, with lots of snow. You could see ice-crystals in the sunrays. Between noon and two in the afternoon you could sit in a deckchair and sunbathe. It was then lovely and warm, but not for long enough to melt the snow. The nights were bitter cold.

As I was walking down to town, I saw in the distance a figure approaching. I couldn't believe my eyes for a moment. Coming up the hill was Vati. What a wonderful surprise! I ran down to meet him. Needless to say, I was so excited, I forgot all about any riding class. Vati and I walked together up to the Guesthaus am Jauchen. We were all so excited and glad that we had made the arrangement with Aunt Trudie to find each other there. Vati had been a prisoner of war. The Americans had released him the previous day. It was wonderful to be a family again, if only Martha could be with us. Thank God the war was over!

Christmas was a very lean time. Money was short and so was the food supply. We didn't give each other any presents, but baked some biscuits and *Streusselkuchen*. We were just grateful that

Chapter Six
The End of the War

we were together and that we survived the war. So many people didn't, on both sides.

Everywhere in Germany the food situation was bad. The shops were almost empty. The whole economy was still in chaos. In contrast to Lofer, where we couldn't get any potatoes, these were easy to get here. We had plenty of potatoes, but nothing to go with them.

The winter was at last over. The snow in the valley was gone, only the mountaintops were still covered with snow. Ingrid and I put on gloves and went into the nearby countryside to collect stinging nettles, fresh young plants. At home we washed them and cook them like spinach. This time I didn't mind the spinach, it had no *grieven* in it and it was something to compliment the dry potatoes.

Sometimes we made fried potatoes. As we had no oil or margarine, we put a few spoonfuls of *Ersatz Kaffee* (imitation coffee) in the frying pan to moisten the potatoes and stop them burning. In those days we appreciated anything edible.

One day Harold came up to the guesthouse to say goodbye to us. He was being sent on some military mission to France and then posted back to America. We were very sad to see him leave.

My job at the pottery was going well. I was getting quite experienced and enjoyed making, painting and glazing lovely items of earthenware. One morning my boss wanted to show me how to mix the clay. He took me to the cellar. There were several stone vessels on the floor. I was shown how much clay powder and how much water to use and mix. I soon realized why he wanted me to mix the clay, which he always used to mix himself first thing in the morning. He kept trying to put his arms round my waist. He also suggested I pose for him nude. He made very nice animal models from clay. Though I was still quite naive, I soon realised his intentions.

As soon as I arrived in the morning before the other staff, he repeatedly tried to put his arms round me. I was not only annoyed (he was a married man in his thirties, but also very upset when he didn't leave me alone. I refused to go back. It meant the end of a lovely job.

Although we enjoyed our stay in Obersdorf with Aunt Trudie,

Chapter Six
The End of the War

we knew we couldn't stay indefinitely. Vati was trying to get back into his profession as a lawyer, but there was no available position in Obersdorf.

One day Mutti and Vati took a trip to Westfalia, where they had friends. Dr K and his wife and two children lived in Soest, a very pretty town near the Moehne Sea, the big lake, which you may remember from the film *The Dam Busters*. A few days later my parents returned. They told us that there was no vacancy for another lawyer yet, but Dr K assured Vati, that next year another lawyer was going to retire and Vati stood a very good chance of taking over that practice.

One of the clothes shops in town wanted hand knitters, so I applied for it and got the job. It wasn't very well paid, but I could take my work home and often I was paid in food items, which was very much appreciated.

There is something else I want to tell you. Somewhere in Obersdorf was a well. There was a seat all around it. One day I had stopped for a moment sitting on the seat. I had just come back from riding and was on my way back to the *Staufen*. A young German sat down next to me. His face was very red, and he had a rather sad expression on his face. He must be suffering from high blood pressure, I thought. He started to talk to me. He told me his wife and two children had been killed. When he went to his parent's house, it was burned out and he didn't know if they were alive or dead. He didn't know why he had come to Obersdorf. Without another word he got up and walked away.

The next day I heard that a young German soldier had fallen from the top of the Nebelhorn. He had multiple fractures and was in hospital. I felt terribly sad. I knew who that person was and why he had fallen. Somehow I even felt guilty for not having been more sympathetic. But there was nothing anyone could have done to help.

Berghaus am Jauchen, Aunt Trudie's guesthouse.

Chapter Seven
Martha's Ordeal

Eventually we were able to contact friends from East Germany through a meeting of East German refugees in Augsburg. Some of my classmates had also been able to flee from the Russian Occupation, while others stayed behind. We heard from Hans F, one of my school friends, who with his family managed to escape after the occupation of Kanth by the Russian troops, that Martha was still in Kanth and that her husband Richard had been killed only days before the end of the war. Richard had been wounded and was being transported along with other casualties in an Army Ambulance clearly marked with the Red Cross on top, when they were attacked by a plane and all were killed.

Today, as I look back on the happenings of that terrible war, I realise that, although we lost everything twice, first in Kanth, and then in Dresden, we were very lucky to be alive and to be together again as a family. If only Martha had come with us.

The conditions in Kanth were horrendous. Our beautiful villa was in ruins. The Russian soldiers took pleasure in throwing our belongings, even furniture, out of the windows and the glass veranda into the garden. They destroyed whatever they could.

Some of the dreadful things that happened in my hometown I can only describe according to what I was told by some of the refugees who were able to flee after the Russian occupation had begun. People were starving, the shops were empty. The Russian Front soldiers were plundering and raping women and young girls. People were suffering from enteritis. They were too weak to fight diseases. Many people got typhoid.

Christa, one of my friends in class, was gang-raped. She killed herself by jumping out of a top floor window onto concrete. Our priest was shot when he threw himself in front of the nuns to protect them. Martha and some other young mothers were able to

Chapter Seven
Martha's Ordeal

ward off Russian rapists by cuddling their babies. One thing was astonishing; even these hardened, ruthless men respected a baby. They didn't harm a woman with a small child. Some young girls hid in cupboards or under mattresses.

Many people got typhoid fever. Martha and her two children, Ingrid and Michael, my godson, were desperately ill with it. Martha crawled on her hands and knees to see to her children, she was so weak. They had very little food, she begged for milk for the children. She lost all her hair. Michael was eighteen-months-old when he died of typhoid.

When the Russian Front Soldiers were replaced by the Russian Regular Army things improved. Gradually Martha and her little daughter got well again, though still very weak. Many people were eventually able to leave and come to the West. They were, including Martha and Ingrid, put on trains (goods wagons). They didn't know where they were being sent and imagined the worst. We had heard so much about people being sent to Siberia. For several days the train was going forward, and sometimes reversing back into a station, but finally they arrived in Friedland, where they stayed in a refugee camp.

Martha's nephew, Gerhard, was injured during the war. He got shrapnel in his head and became totally blind. He was in an East German hospital, but doctors could not remove some of the shrapnel from his brain. He suffered terrible headaches for years. He married the nurse, Liesel, who had looked after him in hospital. They had two sons, whom he never saw. It was all so very tragic. He died in 1952 after many years of pain and sometimes-uncontrollable outbursts of temper.

After a short spell in the refugee camp in Friedland, Martha and her daughter Ingrid were moved on to Leverkusen, near Cologne. Martha got a job in the German chemical factory the Bayer Werke as a cleaner in the laboratories.

We settle in Soest

My parents decided it was time to move on, time to accept that our lives would never be the same again. We were hoping to make a new beginning. We heard that some of the refugees had a chance to resettle in Westfalia. This was the best opportunity we

From left: Top Row: Martha, Mutti, Me, Ingrid (Martha's Daughter) and Gerhard, (Martha's Nephew)
Front: Gerhard's son with my eldest daughter Patricia.
1952.

Chapter Seven
Martha's Ordeal

could have hoped for. A couple of weeks later we were on our way to Westfalia. On our arrival in Soest we were taken to the 'E-Lager' – the refugee camp on the outskirts of the town. Several wooden barracks were built in a large square. The camp official allocated us a fairly large room in one of the barracks, Block 6. There were four put-me-up beds in the room and a table. We managed to get another bed. Vati and Mutti's side of the room, we partitioned off with a sheet. It was all very primitive and I felt sorry for my parents and Oma. There was really no privacy and dignity. For the first few weeks we sat on up turned tea chests, which we obtained from the storeroom.

Our meals we had in a large community hall. I shall always remember the *Stielmus Suppe* – I do not know an English translation; I can only describe it as soup made from the stalks of some kind of greens or cabbage. Sometimes we had Sauerkraut soup.

Gradually things got better. Food supplies improved a little. Vati still had to wait to re-enter his profession. It was another eight months before the lawyer, whose practice Vati was to take over, retired. In the meantime Vati had to find work. He got a job in the Belgian Barracks as a night watchman. One good thing was that Vati got good meals while on duty. But he always brought most of it home for Mutti. No way could Vati enjoy lovely food unless Mutti had it too.

Ingrid was very unhappy that her schooling had been so terribly interrupted for so long. Mutti took Ingrid to Werl, a small town about ten kilometres from Soest. There was a well-known convent, the Ursulinen Kloster. Mutti and Ingrid were invited for an interview. Mutti showed the Mother Superior Ingrid's school reports. Much to our relief Ingrid was immediately accepted to live in the convent and continue her education with the nuns. Ingrid was very excited. The next day her case was packed and Mutti accompanied Ingrid once again to Werl.

I was also very lucky; I got a job in the post office as a telephonist. As I could speak English and French, I was put on the international switchboard, after a brief introduction. I enjoyed my job very much. A few months later I was asked to go with two of my colleagues to Moehne Sea, to work there in the Telephone

Chapter Seven
Martha's Ordeal

Exchange for the British troops stationed at the Moehne Sea. That meant Margret, Helga and I would live there and work alternative shifts.

We shared a large room on the first floor in the Hotel Sommerfeld in Koerbecke, a pretty little village by the Moehne overlooking the lake. Next door to our room was the Telephone Exchange, a small room with one switchboard, a chair and a settee, where we could sleep, whoever was on night duty.

We enjoyed our job and the three of us became good friends. As one of us was always on duty, two of us could go out together. Moehne Sea is a lovely big lake with lots of small, pretty villages and hotels and sandy beaches all around it. The hotels, which were normally occupied by holidaymakers, were now occupied by British soldiers. This was the British Army's Leave Centre. Often the three of us would sit together in our Telephone Exchange. While one of us was on duty, the other one would go downstairs to the restaurant and bring coffee or our meals up to us.

One day we heard that a new British Sergeant was arriving to take charge of the hotels on this side of the Moehne and also the petrol station next door. The hotel owner told us that Colour Sergeant Douglas Gosden, from the Royal Sussex Regiment, was to occupy the room at the end of the corridor. My first recollection of our new 'Boss' was hearing the squeak of his shoes as he passed our exchange. We had a giggle about it and said the shoes must be new and hadn't been paid for, as the saying goes.

When we met Sergeant Gosden we were pleasantly surprised. He was very nice, tall and quite good-looking. My very first encounter with him was when I literally bumped into him. I was in a hurry to catch the bus to go to Soest, when I ran downstairs and straight into his arms, as he was coming up the stairs around the corner. I was very embarrassed and apologised, I felt myself blushing. Later Margret, Helga and I made a bet to see which one of us would eventually make a date with Sergeant Gosden.

On my birthday the three of us were in our exchange, when there was a knock on the door and Sergeant Gosden asked to see me. He wished me 'Happy Birthday' and gave me a bunch of flowers and asked if he could give me a birthday kiss. Again I must have blushed, but he didn't wait for an answer and just

Chapter Seven
Martha's Ordeal

kissed me, Soon Doug and I became a couple. Sometimes we went across the lake to the Sergeants' Mess. As Doug couldn't dance, he didn't mind me dancing with some of his mates, while he played darts and had a few drinks.

I remember the very hot summer, when the lake dried up and we walked across to the other side through the seabed. There were only small patches of water in some places. Whether any fish survived I'm not sure. Fish, mainly pike, must have been re-introduced into the lake after the drought, because the following summer lots of people went fishing again, especially Doug, who was a very keen fisherman, when off duty. Pike was a very tasty fish, but unfortunately full of bones.

Life in the refugee camp in Soest was a far cry from the happy and carefree life we once shared in Selicia not so very long ago, but we made the best of it. The war was over and we were together. Though I worked in Koerbecke, by the Moehne Dam, I went home every two weekends in three, and often for a few hours during the week, especially since Ingrid was in Werl in the convent.

It was common knowledge that it was advisable for the British soldiers not to fraternize with German girls, at least not openly, and not so soon after the end of the war. But many young couples met and fell in love.

Doug and I were no exception. We went out together, to the Sergeant's Mess, sometimes we went to the pictures in the campus. I saw my first English and American films. When I introduced Doug to my family, I was very relieved that they liked him. The only problem was my father asking what profession Doug had in civilian life. When I explained to Vati that Doug was a professional soldier, he was not satisfied with that answer. He insisted to know what Doug had studied in Civilian life. What was Doug going to do when he leaves the Army?

Vati was not very pleased with the answer. He had such high hopes for his daughters. If Doug had been an academic of some decree, Vati would have been well pleased, but an ordinary soldier, no special education; that was something my father resented.

Doug at the Moehne Sea.

Chapter Seven
Martha's Ordeal

Doug and I were very happy in each other's company. When, after a few months Doug applied to the Camp Commandant for permission to marry, he was asked a barrage of questions. Within a week Doug was posted to Berlin. Not because the Army wanted to prevent a soldier marrying a German girl, but mainly to ensure that the people concerned were truly sincere enough – the separation was going to be the test.

We were both very upset. We wrote endless letters to each other. I have still kept all our letters and may enclose a few. My English at the time was not that good, rather funny sometimes.

In Berlin Doug applied, again, for permission to marry a German girl. Once again, every obstacle was put in his way. Finally Doug went to the Army chaplain, who was very helpful. He really got things moving. I had to fill in lots of forms, and obtain written character references from my local priest, and also from the police and a health report from my doctor.

I didn't mind any of this, because it meant that at last things got moving. In the meantime we wrote to each other regularly and also telephoned as often as possible. In March 1950 I visited Doug in Berlin for a two-week holiday. I stayed with friends of Doug's, a married couple, who later were witnesses at our wedding.

To reach Berlin I had to travel through the Russian occupied zone. I needed a special visa and passport. In a small border town, called Helmstedt, all the passengers had to leave the train (without their luggage) and wait on the platform, while the train and luggage were thoroughly searched. After quite a long time the inspection was finished and we were allowed to re-enter the train. The Russian soldiers looked very stern and fearsome. I breathed a sigh of relief when the train moved on again. The same procedure went on, on my way back to Soest.

About eighteen months after meeting Doug, I became a British citizen by deed poll, whereby I swore allegiance to King George the XI. Doug and I got married on 12th August 1950 in Berlin-Charlottenburg, first in the British and again in the German Registry Office. It was a very quiet wedding. Unfortunately Vati didn't approve of my marriage to Doug and therefore didn't come to Berlin. However, Mutti came, against

Chapter Seven
Martha's Ordeal

my father's wishes. It was also attended by a couple of Doug's friends, who were our witnesses. Shortly after, we had a church blessing, which was also a very quiet affair.

We had our first child Patricia, and later Sheila, in the same hospital in Berlin, attended by the same midwife exactly eighteen months apart. Doug was then posted to Sennelager and we followed a week later to live in married quarters. Michael was born about fifteen months later and immediately I sensed something was wrong. Neither English nor German doctors were able to help him and he was moved to the British military hospital in Rinteln, near Hanover. He died aged two-and-a-half months. At the time there was no proper diagnosis given, but after the birth of our daughter Jackie, who had cystic fibrosis, it became apparent that the symptoms were the same.

Doug was demobbed from the army in April 1956, after twenty-two years as a regular soldier. However, before finishing his service, he had to spend the last six months in Chichester, England. During this time Patricia, Sheila and myself stayed in married quarters in Emsworth near Havant. Whilst in Chichester, it was discovered that Doug had tuberculosis of the lung. As his treatment had to be given in the Bevendean Hospital in Brighton, Doug insisted that his family were given accommodation nearby. Fortunately, he had previously placed our names on the housing list, and therefore we were given a house in the Brighton area very quickly.

As I have now finished the chapter of my life in Germany, I feel compelled to show you a letter that my father wrote to my mother, Christmas 1953. It took many years for me to read this letter without getting very emotional. I have now tried to translate it.

Special Festival in Werl

Mutti in the foreground

Patricia with Gerhard's son

Mutti in the refugee camp

The Moehne Sea

Pleasure Boat on the lake

The Moehne Dam

Donnerstag, den 24. Dezember 1953.

Zum Weihnachtsfest 1953.

Meine Ellen!

Zum 27. Male verleben wir heute zusammen das Weihnachtsfest.
Weisst Du noch, als wir zum ersten Male als junge Eheleute in Breslau
auf der Sternstrasse unter dem Christbaum standen? Damals hattest Du
zum ersten Male von meinem vom Vater ererbten Punsch getrunken, und
meine Mutter war auch dabei.

Jetzt sind 27 Jahre darüber vergangen und wir haben allerhand Schönes
und auch viel Schweres zusammen erlebt - und trotzdem waren alle diese
Jahre, ob sie nun im gesicherten Familienkreise stattfanden oder ob
wir unter knappsten Verhältnissen das Christfest begingen, fern von der
alten schönen schlesischen Gebirgsheimat, nicht wunderschön? Wir hatten
uns, das war immer das Entscheidende! Möchtest Du auch nur eins von
diesen vergangenen Jahren missen?

Weisst Du noch, als wir uns in Oberstorf nach dem Zusammenbruch des
Reiches und nach Rückkehr aus meiner Gefangenschaft wiedergefunden
hatten und bei Trude Schmidt-Merz im Gästezimmer froh waren, dass wir
am Christabend einige wenige Gläser Apfelsaft spendiert bekamen, und
unsere beiden Mädels im kalten Klavierzimmer zweistimmig sangen?
Der amerikanische Sergeant hatte mir noch als langentbehrten Genuss
eine dicke Zigarre gespendet! Schenken konnten wir uns natürlich
nichts - als eben unser gegenseitiges Ineinanderaufgehen!
Dann das erste Christfest im E-Lager: Ich hatte von den Belgiern ein
halbes Karepacket bekommen, dass ich als einziges, damals kostbares
Geschenk Dir grossartig spendieren konnte.

Jetzt haben sich die Verhältnisse wenigstens so einigermassen ge-
klärt und wir sind darüber nicht mehr so ganz jung geblieben, wenigstens wohl äusserlich, wenn auch unsere Herzen an der inzwischen ver
flossenenen Zeit un angegriffen vorübergingen: wir sind -darüber bi
ich von Herzen froh, immer das Brautpaar geblieben, das wir vor 27
Jahren waren, trotz Stürmen der Zeit, trotz Kindern und Enkeln!
Ich muss nun einmal, da wir ja nie so allein sind, als wenn wir uns

etwas Schriftliches unter die Nase, bzw. das Näschen halten, dir ganz frei von Mann zur Frau seines Herzens bekennen, wie glücklich Du mich immer gemacht hast, immer und immer, ob auch die Zeiten schwer waren oder wir einigermassen sorgenfrei das Fest begehen konnten. Du warst immer meine Frau, mein Kamerad - und wenn es Bummelkamerad war - und mein tapferer Mitkämpfer! Es ist schon so, wie es Richard Voss in den "Zwei Menschen" sagt: der eine Mensch sucht und sucht, ob er die ihn erst zum ganzen Menschen machende Ergäzung seines Menschentums findet. Wir beiden, meine Ellen, sind der ganze Mensch geworden.

Ich glaube sagen zu können, dass wir eine Ehe geführt haben, wie sie Gott, die Natur, die Ethik wollen. Nun sind bereits unserer Kinder gross, erwachsen, unsre Älteste hat bereits wieder Kinder: wir sind Grossmama und Grosspapa geworden! Und sind wir nicht jung geblieben, so jung, als wir waren, als wir uns als Brautleute in unserer schlesischen Gebirgsheimat fanden, so jung, als wir als Eheleute dann in unserer ersten, uns von meiner Mutter überlassenenen , Wohnung auf der Sternstrasse in Breslau unsere ersten glücklichen Zeiten verlebten?

Ich will nicht rührseelig werden, jetzt, da das Alter herannaht, das liegt mir nicht, wie Du ja weisst, aber eines muss und will ich Dir am heutigen Weihnachtsabend sagen: du warst und bist im wahrsten Sinne des Wortes immer mein "Ich" geblieben, ohne das ich nur ein halber Mensch gewesen wäre. Für Deine Tapferkeit in schwersten Tagen, und Dein immerwährendes Aufgehen in mir sage ich Dir aus ganzer Seel Dank.

Ich bleibe ewig

Dein *Wolfgang*

Chapter Seven
Martha's Ordeal

My father's letter to my mother.

Thursday, the 24th December 1953
Christmas 1953

My Ellen!

For the 27th time we are celebrating Christmas together. Do you remember, when we stood under the Christmas tree in Breslau, in Sternstrasse, as a newly married couple? You had just experienced for the first time the taste of my 'Punch', the recipe of which I have inherited from my father. My mother was also present.

Twenty-seven years have passed since and we have lived through many beautiful and also very hard times, and yet all these years, whether they were spent in the security of our happy family circle, or far from our old beautiful home in Selicia, have been wonderful. We always had each other, that was the main thing. Would you want to have only one of those years gone astray?

Do you remember, when we found each other again after the collapse of the German Reich and I returned from having been a prisoner of war? How happy we were at Trude's Guesthouse, and appreciated the few glasses of apple juice we were given on Christmas Eve, and our two girls sang duets in the cold Music Room. The American Sergeant (Harold Lewes) gave me a much-appreciated thick cigar. Giving each other presents was impossible, only each other's loving togetherness. Remember our first Christmas in the refugee camp 'E-Lager'? In the Belgian Barracks I received a gift parcel, which I could present to you as the sole and valuable present.

Now, at last, the situation has improved slightly, but we have not remained as young any longer, at least not outwardly, though our hearts have not been affected adversely. We have remained the newlyweds, for which I am eternally grateful, for twenty-seven years, through the storms of times, and also children and grandchildren.

As we are never really alone, I want to write it down and tell you from the bottom of my heart, how very happy you have always made me, always and always, whether the times were hard, or whether we spent the festive season carefree and without any worries. You were always my wife, my comrade, my cheerful friend and my brave soldier. It is so very true, what Richard Voss wrote in his book Zwei Menschen *(Two people) that the*

Chapter Seven
Martha's Ordeal

> *human being searches and searches to find the missing link to his whole existence; until two people become one in spirit. The two of us, dear Ellen, have become one whole human being.*
>
> *I believe I can honestly say that our marriage was as God, Nature and Ethic has intended. Now our children have grown up, our eldest one has already got children. We have become grandmother and grandfather! And we have remained young, young at heart like we were when we moved into our first home as newlyweds – the apartment in Sternstrasse in Breslau, which my mother had given us. This was the beginning of a happy future.*
>
> *I do not want to sound morbid, that is not my intention, but now, as our old age approaches, I must and will tell you once more on today's Christmas Eve: 'You were and are in the truest sense of the word, always my soul mate. Without you, I would only be half a person. For your bravery in our darkest days, and your steadfast devotion to me, I want to thank you from the bottom of my heart.'*
>
> *I am eternally*
>
> *Yours*
>
> *(Wolfgang)*

122 HOLLINGBURY
TERRACE
BRIGHTON (7)
SUSSEX
ENGLAND

12 AUGUST 49

To whom it may concern

We the undersign are desirous of having Fraeulein Kilen HENNIG of Soest. Who is at present employed by the GPO and is a telephonist at No 3 BAOR Leave Centre, Mohne See- For a holiday in Brighton England for a period of 1 month at the beginning of 1950.

While staying at this address her care and welfare will be looked after by us.

MR & MRS GOSNEY J

Darling

Here are the papers. Please let me have them back soon. Cheerio my sweetheart and remember that I am always thinking of you and always having you.

All my love and kisses from your ever loving sweetheart

Bangay xxxxxxxx
xxxxxxxx
Better on lips than on paper

April 2nd '45
Wednesday.

58 Saunders Road
Anglen 7
Sussex
England

My dearest own Ellen sweetheart. Just a few lines to let you know how I feel. I'm in the very best of health, also happy, dear. That Darling, it will not be long now before you are my Jeannie, wife and own. It brings that great day nearer. Keep smiling darling, never mind, soon.

The weather over at Anglen is very cold, today I went fishing again from the Palace Pier, but I never caught much. Nevermind

Any news my Darling? I think about this all the time, all for news go by close and keep hoping to hear from you soon. Keep smiling and cheerio for now

All my love
a kiss for now
from your own loving and thoughtful husband to be

Jeannie — xxx
xx xx xxxx
xx xxx+
xxxx

ICH HAB DI LIEB MINE KLINE LIEBER.

P Please sweetheart I am sorry to write in the Club only I have forgotten Ulla's address please put it on cover letter

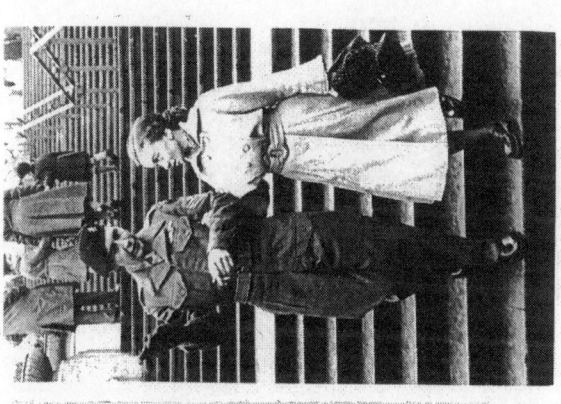

15.2.50.

My dearest only Snuggy!

Thanks to God, I have got some money again, as today is the 15th. The first I bought is this writing-paper. — I am on duty 65 hours and have 6 hours off duty — then night-duty again. Four night ladies "reported". This morning nobody came to release me, as often their friends are with them, they forgot everything. At 2 o'clock p.m. they sent me my lunch. They are celebrating Margrit's birthday. — Colleen I am off-duty once again. I'll go to town to buy some wool a-roll, I'll buy knit a one more frock for me, will look nicer than the first one, also some good material for a coat.

The steps leading to the Aquarium in Brighton

Four Generations

Me about twenty years

My Parents Silver Wedding, 1951

Mutti and Ingrid

The Big Lake in Soest, the oldest town in Westfalia

Printed in Great Britain
by Amazon.co.uk, Ltd.,
Marston Gate.